BUT, IN A LARGER SENSE, WE CAN NOT DEDICATE—WE CAN NOT CONSECRATE—WE CAN NOT HALLOW—THIS GROUND. THE BRAVE MEN, LIVING AND DEAD, WHO STRUGGLED HERE, HAVE CONSECRATED IT, FAR ABOVE OUR POOR POWER TO ADD OR DETRACT. THE WORLD WILL LITTLE NOTE, NOR LONG REMEMBER WHAT WE SAY HERE, BUT IT CAN NEVER FORGET WHAT THEY DID HERE. IT IS FOR US THE LIVING, RATHER, TO BE DEDICATED HERE TO THE UNFINISHED WORK WHICH THEY WHO FOUGHT HERE HAVE THUS FAR SO NOBLY ADVANCED. IT IS RATHER FOR US TO BE HERE DEDICATED TO THE GREAT TASK REMAINING BEFORE US—THAT FROM THESE HONORED DEAD WE TAKE INCREASED DEVOTION TO THAT CAUSE FOR WHICH THEY GAVE THE LAST FULL MEASURE OF DEVOTION—THAT WE HERE HIGHLY RESOLVE THAT THESE DEAD SHALL NOT HAVE DIED IN VAIN—THAT THIS NATION, UNDER GOD, SHALL HAVE A NEW BIRTH OF FREEDOM—AND THAT GOVERNMENT OF THE PEOPLE, BY THE PEOPLE, FOR THE PEOPLE, SHALL NOT PERISH FROM THE EARTH.

W9-BFA-417

LINCOLN

~ IN 3-D ~

AMAZING *and* RARE STEREOSCOPIC
PHOTOGRAPHS OF HIS LIFE AND TIMES

by BOB ZELLER *and* JOHN J. RICHTER

PROLOGUE BY HAROLD HOLZER

CHRONICLE BOOKS

SAN FRANCISCO

Text and anaglyphs copyright © 2010 by Bob Zeller and John J. Richter.

All rights reserved. No part of this book may be reproduced in any form without written permission from the publisher.

Library of Congress Cataloging-in-Publication Data

Zeller, Bob, 1952-
  Lincoln in 3-D / By Bob Zeller and John Richter.
      p. cm.
  Includes bibliographical references.
  ISBN 978-0-8118-7231-7 (hardcover)
  1. Lincoln, Abraham, 1809-1865--Pictorial works.
2. Photography, Stereoscopic. I. Richter, John J. II. Title. III.
Title: Lincoln in three dimensional. IV. Title: Lincoln in 3D.

  E457.6.Z45 2010   2010013792

Manufactured in China

Designed by Trina Hancock

10 9 8 7 6 5 4 3 2 1

Chronicle Books LLC
680 Second Street
San Francisco, California 94107

www.chroniclebooks.com

TABLE OF CONTENTS

❦ PROLOGUE ❧

By Harold Holzer

THOUGH HE LACKED a science education of any kind, Abraham Lincoln—best known as lawyer, politician, writer, and orator—never disguised his passion for technology. He loved astronomy. He developed a keen interest in meteorology. He advocated the development of the railroad not only as a means of bringing the vast United States closer together, but in the hope that transportation could become ever swifter. He meticulously crafted and more than once performed an indulgent but earnest lecture on "Discoveries and Inventions." He even won a patent for his own ingenious, but ultimately impractical, device for buoying heavy vessels over river shoals. He remains the only American president to hold a federal patent for an invention.

Later, as commander in chief, Lincoln embraced military technology with equal ardor: balloon reconnaissance, rifled and wrought-iron cannons, experimental machine guns, breech-loading rifles, steam rams, ironclad warships, humidity-resistant gunpowder, even the use of "incendiary" shells and fluid, a kind of primitive, though deadly, form of napalm. No marksman, and immune to the joys of hunting (he was said to have been repulsed by the sight of blood from the first prey he ever bagged), Lincoln nonetheless enjoyed testing newfangled guns, authorizing experimental weaponry (like the so-called Absterdam projectile— "too good a thing to be lost to the service," he insisted in 1864), or watching in awe as giant artillery hurled shells toward distant targets with breathtaking precision and brutal force. The Civil War, he icily maintained, could not be won with mere "elder-stalk squirts, charged with rose water."

Lincoln's passion for scientific innovation extended, as well, to another technology born and constantly evolving and improving during his own lifetime: photography. Though he always maintained a proper, Victorian-era attitude toward the medium—being careful never to appear too eager, requiring others to usher him to galleries to have his portrait made, and occasionally joshing that the results were nothing more than "sun pictures"— he quickly came to realize the power of their mass production and widespread distribution. "I have not a single one at my control," he replied to one request for his photograph in 1860, "but I think you can easily get one at New-York. While I was there I was taken to one of the places where they get up such things, and I suppose they got my shaddow [*sic*], and can multiply copies indefinitely." Here in just two sentences was Lincoln's complete attitude toward photography in a nutshell: out of modesty (whether real or required by society), he had required someone else to take him to Mathew Brady's studio the day of his career-altering Cooper Union address at New York. The result, he added with self-deprecating humor, was that Brady had captured his "shaddow." But for the admirers who wished to display the image during the presidential campaign to come, Brady's gallery, he well knew, could "multiply copies indefinitely." It did. A year later, in a private moment, Lincoln would admit in the presence of the famous photographer: "Brady and the Cooper Institute made me President." The picture, he was suggesting, had been every bit as influential as the speech.

A COLUMN OF ARMS
Stacked muskets in war-torn Petersburg,
Virginia, in 1865. *(Library of Congress)*

For the rest of his life, Lincoln somehow managed to ensure that his image was duly recorded and widely distributed in all the latest photographic technologies. Once the fashion for daguerreotypes and tintypes had been eclipsed by speedier processes, Lincoln's visage was presented in wall-display-size albumen prints, album-ready cartes de visite, and the vivid, multi-lens-camera stereoscopic views which, like no other medium, brought people and places vividly to life in staggeringly realistic three-dimension.

As he grew his famous whiskers from late 1860 to 1861, Lincoln sat for photographs that traced the progress of his beard for an eager public. When he arrived in Washington for his inauguration, following a widely criticized and personally humiliating secret, late-night dash through a reportedly Lincoln-hostile Baltimore, he combated the resulting caricatured lampoons by sitting in calm dignity for photographer Alexander Gardner in the capital. Shortly before traveling to Gettysburg to deliver his immortal oration at its new soldiers' cemetery, and just weeks before and again, days after, delivering his second inaugural, he made certain he was not only before crowds of people, but before the cameras for an even-wider audience. Somehow he seemed to sense that just as publication of his words would exponentially increase the circulation of his ideas, the reproduction and mass-distribution of his image would supply equally important and widely available visual

SKETCH ARTIST IN THE FIELD
Thirty-four-year-old Alfred R. Waud, the prolific battlefield sketch artist for *Harper's Weekly,* posed for photographer Timothy O'Sullivan in Devil's Den on the Gettysburg battlefield just a few days after the battle. *(Library of Congress)*

accompaniment—something more visceral and emotionally meaningful than mere illustration—that permitted Americans to share his suffering by embracing his aging countenance as an icon.

Lincoln had his own peculiar opinions about how he should be presented in the medium of photography. Before his national prominence, he occasionally posed wearing wrinkled coats and outlandish ties, his hair tousled. When, in August 1863, Gardner took a rather awkward-looking pose of President Lincoln folded uncomfortably in a low chair, left elbow resting uneasily on a thick book, his head propped up by his huge fist, his swallow-tail coat cascading sloppily toward the floor, the subject inexplicably loved the result. "The imperial photograph, in which the head leans upon the hand," he wrote the photographer, "I regard as the best that I have yet seen." A few weeks later, perhaps concerned that others did not share his appreciation for the picture, he was back before Gardner's lens again. This time the results, Lincoln's private secretary cheered, were among the "best" pictures of Lincoln that he had ever seen.

Other media romanticized Lincoln's startling, and later, declining appearance—engravings and lithographs added color and softened the harsh lines incising his face—but photography recorded it accurately, sometimes painfully. And yet the dutiful president, seemingly aware of his obligation to history, never shied away from the camera's unflinching eye. For generations, however, an irresistible legend accompanied what was believed to be the last of his sittings. He had gone to Alexander Gardner's gallery only four days before his assassination, as the story went, and posed for a series of brutally frank pictures showing him more haggard than ever, yet with a long-elusive smile finally flickering on his careworn face, no doubt happy because the war had ended at last. Aware he was capturing a priceless moment, Gardner moved his camera toward the president and took one final close-up. But in the processing room, he mishandled the close-up's glass plate, and it cracked in two above the subject's head. The photographer made but one print—clearly showing the crack. When news of Lincoln's murder reached the public, the picture took on greater meaning still: not only was it Lincoln's last portrait, but it showed an ominous halo of death hovering above his face.

The trouble was, the story proved untrue. A subsequently discovered artist's diary revealed that Lincoln had gone to Gardner's not on April 10 but on February 5. Instead, his last photograph turned out to be a rather bizarre outdoor picture, taken by a Massachusetts lensman named Henry F. Warren on the portico of the White House on March 6, 1865, just two days

CREATING 3-D PORTRAITS (TOP)

Most of the portraits in this book were taken with a camera with four lenses in a square for mass-production purposes. The side-by-side pairs of images from a four-lens camera work together in 3-D. The two card photographs shown here were used together to form the 3-D portrait on page six. *(Stereo photo illustration by John J. Richter)*

A CIVIL WAR-ERA VIEWER (BOTTOM)

The handheld "Holmes-Bates" stereo viewer was the most common device used for viewing 3-D photos in the 1860s. *(Stereo photograph by John J. Richter)*

CATALOGUE

OF

CARD PHOTOGRAPHS,

PUBLISHED AND SOLD BY

E. & H. T. ANTHONY,

501 BROADWAY,

THREE DOORS FROM THE ST. NICHOLAS HOTEL.

NEW-YORK.

NOV., 186

...ins, together with other su...
...own in Europe and Americ...
...LERY."

...gue" will be made daily, a...
1st of every month.

...any time, and copies will...

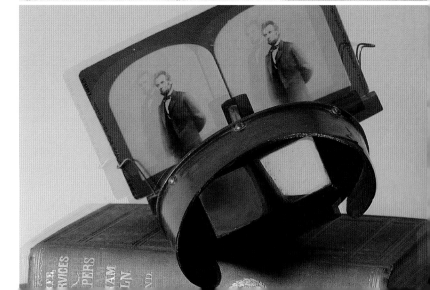

after his second inauguration. It shows Lincoln blinking against a gusty wind and practically sneering in annoyance as he poses. How ironic that a politician who made so many efforts to sit patiently for the cameras, over so many years, with such obvious and enormous benefits to his reputation, should be captured by a photographer for the final time looking impatient and ill-at-ease.

One senses, however, that had Lincoln known that all his pictures would be treasured for so many generations to come, he would have endured this last inconvenience with a bit more equanimity. Certainly, had he lived to see the 3-D results gathered so handsomely in this volume—still startling and enormously appealing even for those of us bombarded by the avalanche of images available on the worldwide Web, camera phones, and podcasts—he would have been thankful for every time he posed. Here, on the pages to come, every bit as dazzling as when the images first appeared, is the unforgettable, unfathomable face of Abraham Lincoln, just as vibrant-looking as when he lived, and became the leading player in a dramatic upheaval we continue to explore with fascination. Here is art married to technology at the highest levels of nineteenth-century achievement, a subject and a process made for each other, and made as well for the ages. To paraphrase Lincoln's own lecture on discoveries and inventions, these astonishingly lifelike pictures still have power, still add "the fuel of interest to the fire of genius."

AS PRESIDENT-ELECT
This studio portrait of Lincoln was taken about a week before he was inaugurated as the sixteenth president of the United States.
(John J. Richter Collection)

LINCOLN SPEECH MEMORIAL (TOP)

Located within the Soldiers' National Cemetery at Gettysburg, Pennsylvania, the Lincoln Speech Memorial was dedicated on January 24, 1912, to honor the president's famous Gettysburg Address. *(Stereo photo by John J. Richter)*

A SCENE FROM THE OLD SOUTH (BOTTOM)

This antebellum plantation scene by Charleston photographers Osborn & Durbec, published here on the printed page for the first time, shows an African American slave holding the horse of a well-to-do South Carolinian as he prepares to board his buggy outside the planter's summer residence in Rockville, South Carolina, in 1860. *(Robin Stanford Collection)*

PHOTOGRAPHERS AT FORT SUMTER (OPPOSITE PAGE)

A group of photographers and assistants pose with an imperial-sized camera on the sandbar next to Fort Sumter in March 1865. *(Library of Congress)*

IN 1839, when photography shouldered its way onto the world stage with a visual splendor unlike anything preceding it, Abraham Lincoln, at thirty, was nurturing a young political career as a third-term legislator in the Illinois House of Representatives while building his new law practice in Springfield, Illinois. Lincoln undoubtedly read newspaper reports about the invention of photography, replete with awe-inspiring descriptions penned by writers who struggled to find words to describe how a photograph looked to a people who had never seen such a thing.

"They are the most remarkable objects of curiosity and admiration, in the arts, that we ever beheld," wrote the editor of *The Knickerbocker* in December 1839 after seeing some of the first photographs (known as "daguerreotypes" for their inventor, Frenchman Louis-Jacques-Mandé Daguerre) on display in New York City. "Their exquisite perfection almost transcends the bounds of sober belief," inventor and painter Samuel F. B. Morse wrote. "It is one of the most beautiful discoveries of the age. No painting or engraving ever approached it."

The new invention was yet another shining achievement of civilization's progress—and another reason for antebellum Americans to marvel at how modern was the time in which they lived. The steam engine was revolutionizing transportation, and the locomotive, also known as the iron horse, was coursing through the countryside, chugging from one city to the next with remarkable speed and ease. In the 1830s, Morse himself had perfected his telegraph, which fired Morse code messages across vast distances like flashes of lightning. And a newfangled machine called a reaper harvested crops faster than an entire crew

It was an age of philosophical enlightenment, too, and religious reaffirmation. Across the country, Americans rededicated themselves to the moral values of their Christian heritage, and so began to look at the inconvenient truth of slavery as a blemish on democracy's lofty ideals. By the 1830s, the issue of involuntary servitude had been a matter of debate in North America for at least eighty years. The tone of the discussion sharpened, however, when a Massachusetts social reformer, William Lloyd Garrison, began to frame slavery in a religious context, insisting that owning slaves was a sin against God. In 1831, Garrison established a weekly newspaper, *The Liberator*, devoted to the eradication of slavery, and, through it, helped launch the abolitionist movement. The South, whose agricultural economy was dependent on slave labor, held up Garrison as a criminal, and such rancor grew as years and then decades passed.

As the slavery pot simmered on the back burner, an enterprising young daguerreian artist named Nicholas H. Shepherd arrived in the western frontier in 1845 to open one of the first daguerreotype galleries in Springfield, Illinois. Abraham Lincoln and his young wife, Mary, were among his early customers, donning their finest clothes one day in 1846 before sitting in front of the camera, one after the other, each gazing into the lens with the same resolute countenance. In 1847, Lincoln was off to Washington to serve

A PHOTOGRAPHER IN THE FIELD

Mathew Brady, one of the Civil War's greatest photographers, produced photos and stereo views throughout the conflict. His studio's work includes this 1864 scene of Butler's Signal Tower at Cobb's Hill near Petersburg, Virginia, showing a Brady & Co. photographic darkroom wagon and wet plate accessories. (*Library of Congress*)

his first and only term in Congress, where his cause was not slavery—not yet, anyway—but opposition to the Mexican War.

Eight years passed before the next known photograph was taken of Lincoln in 1854; visits to photography galleries back then were extra-special occasions, and most nineteenth-century Americans were photographed only a few times, especially in those early years. By 1857, when Lincoln was photographed for the third time, he was head and shoulders deep into the slavery issue and on the cusp of gaining a national reputation for his eloquent speeches on the thorny issue. While not favoring its outright abolition, Lincoln believed slavery was morally wrong, and he was a staunch opponent of its expansion. His skill in articulating his views captured a wide audience in the North and an equally wide audience—fueled by unmitigated contempt—in the South. His fame, or infamy, grew by leaps and bounds. In four short years, an unheralded one-term congressman from the frontier would vault over a gaggle of better-known politicians and land in the White House itself.

CONFEDERATE DARKROOM

Southern photographers in Charleston were the first to make images of the Civil War when they photographed Fort Sumter and other sites after the fort's surrender in April 1861. This scene from Morris Island shows the Trapier Mortar Battery, which fired 1,300 shells at Fort Sumter. In the background sits the portable developing tent of photographers Osborn & Durbec. (Robin Stanford Collection)

The photographic image played a significant role during Lincoln's unlikely ascent, and from 1857 on, the number of images of him would multiply until he had become, at the time of his death in 1865, one of the most photographed men in America. Ultimately, at least 150 different photographs were taken of our sixteenth president, and the fact that thirty-five of them were created during the presidential campaign year of 1860—more than were taken in any other year of his life—underscores Lincoln's well-tuned political instincts and his understanding of how effective the photograph could be as a tool for communication and recognition.

By March 1861, when Abraham Lincoln became president, the country had split itself apart over slavery, while the photograph had evolved into new forms that expanded its role in American culture. The outmoded daguerreotype had been rendered obsolete—like the film camera today—by cheaper, easier-to-make photographs. The new craze became paper photographs pasted onto cards. The card photograph, or carte de visite, was created using a glass-plate negative, which was exposed and developed, and then placed on a piece of light-sensitive photographic paper and bathed in sunlight. The photo paper, after being developed, was trimmed and then pasted to a thin piece of card stock. A single negative could be used to print four images, or a hundred, or thousands when it came to images of Lincoln and other notables.

Even more sensational was the image known as a stereograph, or stereo view, which was a photograph viewed in 3-D through a stereoscope, or stereo viewer—another 1830s invention. "The first effect of looking at a good photograph through the stereoscope is a surprise such as no painting ever produced," the essayist Oliver Wendell Holmes wrote in 1859. "The mind feels its way into the very depths of the picture. The scraggy branches of a

STEREO FACTORY (THIS PAGE)
The glass-plate negative, introduced in 1851, allowed for the mass-production of stereo-view cards. In this hand-colored view taken around 1860 in France, workers trim and paste prints for card photographs and stereo views. *(Jeffrey Kraus Collection)*

STEREO SHOP (OPPOSITE TOP)
The D. Appleton & Co. stereoscopic emporium on Broadway in New York City—shown in this hand-colored view taken around 1865—was the video store of Civil War America. The stereograph provided a photographic viewing experience that entertained the masses decades before the invention of movies and television. *(Courtesy of Ron Labbe)*

PHOTO EXHIBIT (OPPOSITE BOTTOM)
Visitors to the photography exhibition at the London International Exposition of 1862 saw a wide range of photograph sizes and formats as well as different types of stereo viewers, including a floor-standing model next to the third partition. *(Bob Zeller Collection)*

tree in the foreground run out at us as if they would scratch our eyes out." Before the rise of the stereo view, photography was largely limited to the creation of photographic keepsakes of family and friends. With the advent of mass-marketed stereo views in the late 1850s, and with Holmes's invention of a simple, handheld stereoscope, photography now could also provide a photographic viewing experience. You could take a 3-D tour of the world while sitting in the parlor of your own home. Before movies and television, the stereo view was the closest thing to video that nineteenth-century Americans had. It was the first mass-marketed form of visual home entertainment, and the conflict provided boundless new stereographic opportunities.

LINCOLN IN 1865 (TOP)
This vignette of Lincoln is from a photo taken by government photographer Lewis Emory Walker, probably in early February, 1865. *(Jeffrey Kraus Collection)*

ATLANTA SCENE IN 1864 (OPPOSITE PAGE) & STEREO VIEWER DETAIL (BOTTOM)
Stereo views made their way even to the battlefronts of the war. Just days before the Union Army torched the city of Atlanta in November 1864, Union soldiers under Gen. William Tecumseh Sherman relaxed on Whitehall Street in downtown Atlanta by taking turns peering at 3-D photos in a four-person commercial stereoscopic viewer on a tripod. *(Library of Congress)*

Thus, on the eve of the Civil War, Americans were presented with a new way to see war. The tall bluffs of the Hudson River Valley and the majestic Niagara Falls were enchanting, but people hungered for war news back then just as they devour news today, and the stereo view was a spectacular new visual way to bring actual scenes from the battlefields and the seats of power into American homes. With the rise of mass-marketed photographs, the Lincoln presidency would become the first presidency that was well documented by the camera, most often by the twin-lens camera of the stereo photographer. The Washington that Lincoln knew—the White House, the unfinished Capitol, the great public buildings, the forts that ringed the city—was documented with the depth-filled vividness that only a 3-D photograph can provide. Those same stereo cameras also recorded the war's battlefields, sometimes still fresh with the dead who fell there, the generals who won and lost those battles, and the men who did the fighting, creating a visual legacy that still captivates and moves us today, almost 150 years later.

By the thousands they were printed, those curious little cards with side-by-side photographs, and by the thousands they filtered into American homes, giving Americans a 3-D glimpse of far-off worlds. So it was in the parlor of a home in Springfield, where a stereo viewer sat on a table for the entertainment of the family and the guests of Mr. and Mrs. Abraham Lincoln. The family would soon leave this home, and Lincoln himself would never come back to it.

INSIDE "STEREO CENTRAL"
This is the interior of the Broadway headquarters of the E. & H. T. Anthony & Company, the leading seller of card photographs, stereo views, and photographic supplies during the Civil War. Tabletop and handheld stereo viewers are on display in the foreground.
(Jeffrey Kraus Collection)

AN UPSET
VICTORY

Chapter 01

ON FEBRUARY 11, 1861, a train festooned with flags and streamers chugged out of Springfield, Illinois, and clattered east, running a gauntlet of cheering, flag-waving citizens as it carried Abraham Lincoln to the White House. He was an unlikely president. A westerner, tall and homely, he had a "lean, lank, indescribably gawky figure," wrote journalist Henry Villard, and "an odd-featured, wrinkled, inexpressive, and altogether uncomely face."

BROADWAY IN 1860
The E. & H. T. Anthony & Company was on the cutting edge of photo technology in 1860 with its "instantaneous view," a stop-action photo with a 1/40th of a second exposure that froze omnibuses in motion on Broadway, even in the poor light of a rainy day. "No visitor should leave New York without some of them to astonish friends at home," exclaimed an Anthony advertisement.
(Bob Zeller Collection)

Captivated by politics at a young age, Lincoln taught himself law, passed the bar examination, and began practicing law in Illinois. He lost his first political campaign for a seat in the state general assembly in 1832. He was twenty-three years old. A quarter century would pass before Lincoln burst upon the national political scene in 1858 during his debates with Stephen Douglas in their race for the U.S. Senate. Though he lost the election to Douglas, the name *Lincoln* and the words he spoke were being printed in newspapers from coast to coast.

Lincoln was unmatched as a writer and public speaker. When he took command at a speaker's lectern, his awkward appearance seemed to vanish, and the soaring power of his oratory deeply moved people. He electrified his Northern audiences with his unequivocal stand against the spread of slavery; the same words sent a cold chill coursing through Southern veins.

In the formative years of Lincoln's career, while he was building a law practice in Springfield, the ugly canker of slavery was forcing its way to the surface of American political life. Starting in the early 1830s with the establishment of antislavery newspapers and abolition societies in the North, the movement to abolish an American's right to own and enslave another human being grew in size, sound, and influence through the 1840s and 1850s. To the South, slavery was an economic necessity—a right that had survived unmolested when the new country articulated its principles in the U.S. Constitution. By the late 1850s, slavery was the issue that dwarfed all others.

In 1859, Lincoln stumped the Midwestern states (then called the West), stirring the masses with his orations in Council Bluffs, Iowa; Columbus and Cincinnati, Ohio; Indianapolis, Indiana; Milwaukee, Wisconsin; Chicago, Illinois; Leavenworth, Kansas; and other cities. He was invited to come to New York and his watershed speech at the Cooper Union on February 27, 1860, combined with a flattering photograph taken the same day by photographer Mathew Brady and widely copied and distributed, cemented his standing as the rising star of Republican politics in the North, and anathema to the South.

The Republican Convention of 1860 was in Chicago, and former New York Governor William Seward was the frontrunner among several candidates. Lincoln threw his hat in and emerged as everyone's second choice. He skillfully exploited the others' weaknesses, sold himself as the compromise candidate, and achieved an upset victory on the third ballot. After winning the nomination, Lincoln followed the custom of the time and did not publicly campaign—an unthinkable strategy today. He lay low in Springfield, wrote letters to bolster his cause, and let others such as Seward do the campaigning.

Fewer than four of ten Americans voted for Abraham Lincoln in November 1860; he wasn't even on the ballot in nine Southern states. But the hopelessly divided country split its vote between Lincoln and three other candidates. Lincoln carried eighteen of the thirty-three states, sweeping the more populous North, and won a majority of the all-important electoral votes. His election outraged the South and triggered a winter of secession. South Carolina removed itself from the United States on December 20, 1860, soon followed by Mississippi, Florida, Alabama, Georgia, Louisiana, and—ten days before Lincoln's departure from Springfield—Texas as well.

The upper South—Virginia, North Carolina, Kentucky, Tennessee, and Maryland—hung in the balance as Lincoln and his family slowly made their way east in the luxury of the presidential car, with its dark polished furniture, thick carpet, and tasseled, crimson curtains. But mortal danger lurked in those final miles to Washington, DC, or so said the incoming president's security detail. Wearing a soft felt cap instead of his trademark black top hat, Lincoln was spirited onto a night train in Philadelphia and conveyed secretly through secession-minded Maryland to the nation's capital. Lincoln lay doubled up in a too-short berth, unable to sleep, and in the middle of the night in Baltimore, listened to a drunk sing "Dixie" on the platform

JEFFERSON DAVIS AT BEAUVOIR

No stereo views are known to exist of Jefferson Davis as president of the Confederacy, but this view from 1884 or 1885 shows Davis and his wife, Varina (right), as proud grandparents at Beauvoir, their home on the Mississippi Gulf Coast at Biloxi. Davis lived until 1889. *(Michael Griffith Collection)*

AFTER THE LONG JOURNEY

Still appearing tired after his long trip from Springfield, Illinois, to Washington, DC, President-elect Lincoln sat for these two studio portraits by Alexander Gardner at Mathew Brady's studio on February 24, 1861, just one day after arriving in the capital. Pressed for time, Lincoln looked at his pocket watch just before the lower photo was taken and holds it, still open, in his right hand. *(John J. Richter Collection)*

FREDERICK DOUGLASS (OPPOSITE PAGE)

Frederick Douglass, shown in this post-war image, was twenty years old when he escaped his life as a slave in Maryland in 1838. He became a leading abolitionist and lecturer and, during the war, fought for enlistment and equal treatment of black soldiers. He twice met with President Lincoln in the White House and was profoundly impressed. *(Library of Congress)*

AN UPSET

Chapter 01

at Camden Station. Lincoln was mocked for, and embarrassed by, his stealthy Washington arrival at 6 A.M. on February 23.

Soon after arriving, the president-elect took a seat under the skylight of Mathew Brady's Washington photographic studio, rested his left arm on a small parlor table, and posed for five photographs, scarcely moving between exposures. Lincoln has a distant, disengaged look in the photos from this sitting, as if lost in thought, or perhaps just exhausted from the endless hand shaking and speech making on a 1,904-mile train trip, culminated by a sleepless final night.

Years later, a youthful Brady associate, George H. Story, recalled the sitting, saying that Gardner had come to his room and asked him to pose Lincoln. "When I entered the room the President was seated in a chair wholly absorbed in deep thought," Story said. "I said in an undertone to the operator, 'bring your instrument here and take the picture.'" Lincoln's first sitting in Washington was done for *Harper's Weekly,* which published an engraving of one of the images on April 27, 1861.

Lincoln took the oath of office under clear skies on a cool March 4, 1861, standing under a simple, canopied, wooden platform erected on the front steps of the Capitol, with the unfinished dome above him looking like two layers of a wedding cake. He faced east, but his inaugural address was directed to the South. "I have no purpose, directly or indirectly, to interfere with the institution of slavery in the states where it exists," he declared. "In your hands, my dissatisfied fellow countrymen, and not in mine, is the momentous issue of civil war. The government will not assail you. You can have no conflict without being yourselves the aggressors."

"We are not enemies, but friends," Lincoln concluded. "We must not be enemies. Though passion may have strained, it must not break our bonds of affection. The mystic chords of memory, stretching from every battle-field, and patriot grave, to every living heart and hearthstone, all over this broad land, will yet swell the chorus of the Union, when again touched, as surely they will be, by the better angels of our nature."

Waiting for him at the White House, though, was a fiendishly tricky dilemma that might as well have been the work of the devil for the problems it posed.

LINCOLN'S FIRST INAUGURATION

Below the unfinished dome of the Capitol building, Abraham Lincoln took the oath of office as the sixteenth president of the United States. Far behind the crowd, avid amateur photographer Montgomery C. Meigs, soon to be quartermaster general of the Union army, took this stereo photograph of the ceremony. *(Courtesy of the Center for Civil War Photography)*

AN UPSET

VICTORY

Chapter 01

SOUTHERN ARTILLERY MILITIA

Most of the documentary images and stereo
views by Southern photographers were taken
before the war and during its early months,
when chemicals and photo paper were still
readily available. Here, a Confederate artillery
militia unit in Charleston poses for the stereo
camera of photographers Osborn & Durbec.
(Robin Stanford Collection)

PLANTATION LIFE IN DEPTH

Slavery existed in America for more than 250 years, fueling the plantation system that was at the heart of the South's agrarian economy. Some of the most compelling and dramatic early Southern photos are scenes of plantation life. In early 1866, Beaufort, South Carolina, photographer Erastus Hubbard traveled to nearby St. Helena Island and Port Royal Island to make stereo photographs at several plantations. He also photographed a black school created in 1862 by Philadelphia native Laura Towne after Union forces occupied the area. "The wretched hovels with their wooden chimneys and the general squalor showed the former misery" of slavery, Towne wrote in her diary, describing the shacks where the ex-slaves lived. "We saw one woman whose two children had been whipped to death, and Mr. Wells said there was not one who was not marked up with welts." Hubbard's plantation views are distinctive for their exaggerated "hyper-stereo" three-dimensional effect. Most of the images presented here are published for the first time on the printed page.

EX-SLAVES AND THEIR BABIES
Five young African American women, all former slaves, pose with their babies in front of their homes on the T. J. Fripp plantation.
(Robin Stanford Collection)

HARVESTING COTTON BY HAND
(PREVIOUS PAGES ON LEFT)
African American ex-slaves were photographed on their way to the cotton field on the D. F. Thorpe plantation on St. Helena Island, South Carolina. *(Robin Stanford Collection)*

A ROW OF SLAVE CABINS
(PREVIOUS PAGES ON RIGHT)
Slave quarters, still occupied by now-free African Americans, stretch across a field at Perry Clear Point, Port Royal Island, South Carolina, in early 1866. *(Robin Stanford Collection)*

THE BIG HOUSE (OPPOSITE PAGE)
Erastus Hubbard's stereo camera captured the "Big House" on the T. J. Fripp plantation, St. Helena Island, South Carolina. It still stands today. *(Robin Stanford Collection)*

THE PENN SCHOOL
(FOLLOWING PAGE ON LEFT)
Laura Towne's Penn School on St. Helena Island, South Carolina, is shown here in early 1866, soon after the long-awaited new school bell arrived from the North and was installed in the bell tower. The school still exists today as Penn Center and the original bell is displayed at the center's museum. *(Robin Stanford Collection)*

WAIST DEEP IN COTTON
(FOLLOWING PAGE ON RIGHT)
Gullah women of Mt. Pleasant, South Carolina, prepare sea island cotton for the ginning mills on the Alex. Knox plantation near Charleston in this ca. 1874 photograph by George N. Barnard. *(Robin Stanford Collection)*

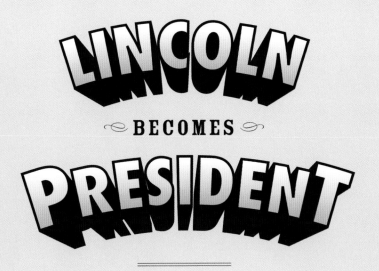

LINCOLN

⟨⟩ BECOMES ⟨⟩

PRESIDENT

Chapter **02**

THE LINCOLNS danced and socialized past midnight at the "Palace of Aladdin," which held the inaugural ball, and finally Abraham took leave of his wife, Mary, who remained, and returned by coach to the White House. The new president would never forget the moment he stepped into his office: "The first thing that was handed to me after I entered this room, when I came from the inauguration, was the letter from Maj. Anderson saying that their provisions would be exhausted before an expedition could be sent to their relief."

WHERE THE CIVIL WAR STARTED

This Osborn & Durbec image shows Southerners on the parapet of Fort Sumter just days after its surrender on April 13, 1861, by its Union defenders, who had battled for thirty-four hours using some of the guns seen here. The piece in the foreground apparently was disabled by a misfire, not Southern shells. *(Robin Stanford Collection)*

At the entrance to the harbor of Charleston, South Carolina, the womb of secession, a federal army major, Robert Anderson, was holed up with his eighty-five men in Fort Sumter, which he had surreptitiously occupied six days after South Carolina seceded. Outraged, the seceded state's leaders demanded his withdrawal. They considered the fort Southern property once the state left from the Union. Anderson refused to depart, squatting defiantly in the federal installation through January and February, as food dwindled and tension grew. The fort would run out of provisions in six weeks, Anderson now reported. He estimated it would take twenty thousand men to resupply and reinforce the garrison. Should Lincoln do that and risk a Southern attack? Or should he order Anderson to withdraw?

Day after day, the commander in chief ruminated, unable to decide. His new cabinet, largely made up of former opponents, was divided. Meanwhile, an endless flow of office seekers lined the halls of the White House, which was open to the public then,

believing only an audience with Lincoln himself would suffice. Lincoln considered public sessions his duty and endured the ordeal of seeing the petitioners one by one.

After two weeks, Lincoln still could not decide what to do about Fort Sumter, so he postponed any action and sent an emissary south on a fact-finding mission. Lincoln later told a friend that "all the troubles and anxieties of his life" failed to equal those he faced at this time. On March 29, Lincoln finally made a decision: He told his cabinet that he would launch a naval expedition to resupply Fort Sumter but only with nonmilitary supplies. The new Confederate States of America responded by formally demanding on April 11 that Anderson evacuate. He refused. At 4:30 A.M. the next day, cannons boomed, and Confederate shells pounded the fort. The Civil War had begun.

When Anderson surrendered after thirty-four hours of shelling, the news thrilled the South, but outraged and unified the North. Lincoln called for 75,000 volunteers, and every state immediately overfilled its quota. In New York on April 20, one of the city's largest crowds ever filled Union Square to support the government.

THEY BOMBARDED FORT SUMTER

These Confederate guns and artillerymen at Fort Moultrie hurled shells into Fort Sumter during the war's first engagement. Combatants on both sides fired more than 4,000 rounds of artillery before Union Maj. Robert Anderson hoisted a white hospital bed sheet over Sumter to signal his surrender. Miraculously, no one was killed or seriously wounded. *(Bob Zeller Collection)*

Chapter 02

CONTEMPLATING HIS TROUBLES (TOP)

Lincoln appears deep in thought in this candid pose taken during his second visit to the Brady gallery in Washington, DC, probably in the spring of 1862. The exact date is lost to history. *(John J. Richter Collection)*

THE GREAT UNION MEETING (BOTTOM)

After evacuating Fort Sumter, Maj. Robert Anderson went to New York City, where on April 20, 1861, he spoke at the "Great Union Meeting" in Union Square, shown in this E. & H. T. Anthony & Company instantaneous view. "The people of this great town were there in full force, realizing the emergency, and ready to maintain the Union that has made New York what it is," wrote a correspondent of the *Illustrated London News. (Robin Stanford Collection)*

WHITE HOUSE ENCAMPMENT (OPPOSITE PAGE)

After Fort Sumter's surrender, Washington, DC, remained largely unprotected for eleven tense days. Finally the blue-blooded Seventh New York Regiment and other troops arrived by train after fixing tracks destroyed by secessionists in Maryland. Troops assigned to guard the White House built these temporary quarters on the grounds in 1861. *(Bob Zeller Collection)*

Lincoln could consider himself fortunate to have the North's universal support, because almost nothing else went right in the first days of the conflict. Washington itself was almost wholly unprotected and unprepared for war, and when Virginia seceded on April 17, the threat was as easy to see as the Confederate flag defiantly flying above the Marshall House in Alexandria. Regiments of Virginians were said to be marching toward Washington, and the confident demeanor of the Southerners still in the capital left Northerners unnerved, especially after the Confederate secretary of war predicted that the "Stars and Bars" would fly over the United States Capitol by the first of May. Artillery units were placed at the Long Bridge over the Potomac River, and scattered, sundry militia units and guards were stationed at key public buildings. The first reinforcements— five companies of Pennsylvania troops—finally arrived at the train station on April 18, while Kansas Sen. Jim Lane took up quarters "in picturesque bivouac on the brilliant-patterned velvet carpet" of the East Room at the White House with about sixty "Frontier Guards" he assembled from the Illinoisans and Kansans in the capital.

The next day, though, the Sixth Massachusetts was attacked by a mob in Baltimore and at least four soldiers and nine civilians died—the war's first casualties. Virginia troops captured the weapons armory at Harper's Ferry, while Marylanders burned the bridges around Baltimore, cutting off the capital from the north. On April 20, the federals abandoned the crucial Navy Yard in Norfolk as the torrent of bad news intensified.

Washington became a city under siege. The city's hotels emptied, while shops closed their doors and boarded their windows. The price of flour doubled in two days. The State Department's clerks became its guards. Sandbag breastworks were thrown up on the porticoes of the Treasury Building, which was designated a bastion of last resort for the president, while its basement was filled, not with money, but with two thousand barrels of flour. Days passed, and no more help came from the North. The vaunted Seventh New York Regiment was said to be on its way. Troops were boarding ships in Philadelphia to avoid the Baltimore bottleneck. But there was no sight of any of them.

Lincoln paced the White House floors, and from the upper windows he peered down the Potomac, hoping to see ships bearing soldiers. "Why don't they come?" he anguished. "Why don't they come?" He invited the wounded soldiers of the Sixth Massachusetts to the White House and told them with bitter mirth, "I begin to believe that there is no North. The Seventh Regiment is a myth . . . You are the only real thing."

The Seventh Regiment finally arrived the following day, and as they marched to the White House, a thousand strong in crisp gray uniforms, cheers of gratitude rained down upon them from citizens lining Pennsylvania Avenue. Troops from Rhode Island and Massachusetts showed up the day after. Soon they would appear by the thousands, including the rowdy New York First Fire Zouaves, headed by Col. Elmer Ellsworth, Lincoln's beloved

KEY CROSSROADS (OPPOSITE PAGE)
Centreville, Virginia, situated on a high ridge about 20 miles west of Washington, was a strategically important town that was used as a supply depot by both sides, depending on who occupied it. Seen here is the Stone Church, used as a hospital after the battles at Bull Run in 1861 and 1862. (Library of Congress)

THE MARSHALL HOUSE (TOP)
ELLSWORTH'S BLOODY UNIFORM
(OPPOSITE PAGE)

One of President Lincoln's closest friends,
Col. Elmer Ellsworth, was the first Union
officer to die in the Civil War. After Ellsworth,
the organizer and commander of the New York
First Fire Zouaves, was gunned down at the
Marshall House in Alexandria, Virginia, on
May 24, 1861, his blood-spattered uniform was
put on display at a fair in New York City to
benefit the Sanitary Commission. (*Library of
Congress; John J. Richter Collection*)

RECRUITING ON BROADWAY (BOTTOM)

In May 1861, an E. & H. T. Anthony & Company
photographer aimed an instantaneous camera
from a second-floor window at the company's
New York offices to capture this stop-action
photo of Broadway. Seen from the back, a huge
recruiting banner spanning the thoroughfare
calls for "Scotchmen for the Union" to join the
Seventy-ninth New York Regiment. (*Jeffrey
Kraus Collection*)

young friend and former employee. On May 24, when Union troops captured Alexandria, Virginia, Ellsworth took his Zouaves to the Marshall House, where he snatched the Rebel flag from the roof and was shot to death by the owner. A grief-stricken Lincoln had the body brought to the White House to lie in state in the East Room.

The first major battle came two months later at Manassas, Virginia, when a confident Union army marched out and engaged the Confederates in the First Battle of Bull Run. The War Department telegraph at first clicked out encouraging reports, and Lincoln decided to take his usual afternoon carriage ride. But as he toured the city, fortunes changed on the battlefield, and an expected Union victory became a shocking rout, sending the entire army, mixed in with the hundreds of civilian spectators who had traveled out to see the spectacle, fleeing back toward Washington in a panic. Lincoln did not sleep that night, but he did not lose his nerve, either, and sat up writing a memo to reorganize the army and pick up the pieces. The defeat at Bull Run, though, was but a harbinger of things to come.

HENRY HOUSE HILL (OPPOSITE PAGE)
The remains of Judith Henry's home are scattered on Henry House Hill after the First Battle of Bull Run in Manassas, Virginia. This was the war's first land battle. Judith Henry was killed as shells obliterated her house. Photographer George N. Barnard, working for photographer Mathew Brady, took this image in March 1862, eight months after the battle. *(Library of Congress)*

A FAMILY IN CAMP (TOP)

Although women and children were usually not fixtures in Union camps, this soldier in the Thirty-first Pennsylvania Infantry posed with his family in late 1861 or early 1862 outside his tent on Queen's Farm near Fort Slocum in northeast District of Columbia. *(Library of Congress)*

THE RAVAGES OF WAR (BOTTOM)

The Orange & Alexandra Railroad was one of the most contested railroads of the Civil War. This photo from the summer of 1862 shows destroyed rolling stock at Manassas Junction, an immensely important hub that linked rail lines to Richmond, Washington, and the Shenandoah Valley. *(Library of Congress)*

STANDOFF AT SUDLEY FORD (OPPOSITE PAGE)

Imagine what it must have been like to have been one of these Southern children, facing off against Yankee cavalry at Sudley Ford. This photograph was taken by George N. Barnard on the northern part of the Bull Run battlefield in March 1862. *(Library of Congress)*

1862

AND THE BATTLE OF

ANTIETAM

Chapter 03

TO THE TASK of regrouping the shattered Army of the Potomac, Lincoln brought Gen. George Brinton McClellan, a popular officer who was known to be a skillful organizer. McClellan quickly whipped the army into shape but then did nothing with it. His sole initiative in 1861 came in October, when a small Union expedition crossed the Potomac at Ball's Bluff, Virginia, and was routed near the tall banks along the river. Tears and sorrow returned to the White House, for among the forty-nine Union dead was Col. Edward Baker, a United States senator from Oregon, and the only senator ever killed in battle. Baker was an old Lincoln friend and colleague from their days together in the Illinois legislature. The Lincolns thought so highly of him that they had named their second son Edward (who died in 1850 at age three) in his honor.

BURNSIDE BRIDGE
Burnside Bridge on Antietam Creek looked surprisingly tranquil four days after the battle.
(Library of Congress)

Throughout the winter of 1861–1862, Lincoln fretted and cajoled and wheedled and waited on McClellan to move against the Rebels, only to be snubbed and ignored by the insolent general, whose nickname, among others, was "The Young Napoleon." Lincoln finally forced McClellan into Virginia by direct order, but the Confederate troops pulled back toward Richmond, and the Union army did not pursue.

Lincoln's responsibilities as president included not only his overarching duties as commander in chief but also an endless flow of administrative tasks and seemingly countless appointments. He juggled these while also raising a family and tending to the emotional needs of his temperamental wife. Despite Mary Lincoln's neediness and high-strung disposition, the Lincolns were devoted to each other and doted on their children to the point of spoiling them. Their oldest son, Robert, was off at Harvard. But their other two children, eleven-year-old William Wallace, known as Willie, and eight-year-old Thomas, called "Tad," had the run of the White House, and their squeals of laughter and spirited rambunctiousness lightened the mood and brought joy to their parents in a dwelling otherwise filled with tumult and tension.

The new year of 1862 brought a January of sleet and snow, spawning a rash of illnesses across the city. Smallpox and typhoid fever were almost epidemic on some blocks, and illness found its way into the White House, where little Willie, a serious and smart boy, developed a fever after taking a pony ride in foul weather. Tad soon became ill, too, but while Tad was able to recover, Willie's condition worsened. He died on February 20, 1862.

The war, the political infighting, the sober duties of the nation's highest office—all of it now paled in the face of the sadness and grief that overwhelmed the first family. Mary was inconsolable and remained in bed for three weeks. She did not attend the White House funeral. Her husband, however, could not avoid the daily glut of duties that piled up on the desk of his office on the second floor of the White House. Could it get any worse? Even before Willie's fatal illness, the winter months had brought Lincoln to the brink of despondency as he struggled under the weight of an unsettled populace, a bickering Cabinet, a dissatisfied Congress, and a commanding general who was chronically insubordinate.

In the spring of 1862, McClellan finally moved his army down the Chesapeake Bay to the James River peninsula in Virginia to face off against Richmond. Lincoln, starved for any action, had quickly assented to the plan. The Rebel army that came to engage the Yankees fell back toward the capital city on May 3,

and McClellan followed, cautiously. A Confederate surprise attack on May 31 triggered the Battle of Seven Pines, or Fair Oaks, but the Union lines held, and the Confederate commander, Gen. Joseph E. Johnston, was wounded. His replacement was Gen. Robert E. Lee.

On June 25, more than three months after he had embarked for Virginia, McClellan was near Richmond and ready to begin his offensive in earnest. Thus began the Seven Days' Battles. Bloody clashes at Mechanicsville, Gaines' Mill, Savage Station, and Frayser's Farm forced McClellan's army into retreat. Only a gallant Union stand at Malvern Hill prevented a full-scale debacle. McClellan withdrew to Harrison's Landing, ending the Union threat to Richmond, and Lincoln's general-in-chief,

SAVAGE STATION (TOP)
The wounded of the Sixteenth New York who fell at the Battle of Gaines' Mill on June 27, 1862, during the Peninsula Campaign, appear in all manner of suffering in this James Gibson photograph taken at a field hospital outside a farmhouse at Savage Station, Virginia. Most of these men were captured two days later in a massive Confederate counterattack. (Library of Congress)

ON THE DECK OF THE MONITOR (BOTTOM)
The USS Monitor's famous standoff with the CSS Virginia was one of the most famous naval engagements of the Civil War. On July 9, 1862, four months after the fight, photographer James Gibson photographed the ironclad, showing its shell-pocked turret. (Library of Congress)

Henry W. Halleck, ordered the Army of the Potomac back to Alexandria on August 3.

The next initiative was another complete disaster. Union Gen. John Pope was all too eager to throw his Army of Virginia against Confederate forces. The battle again came at Bull Run, and produced the same result. As the remnants of Pope's shattered army streamed back into Washington, Lincoln sighed to Quartermaster Gen. M. C. Meigs: "Pope is licked, and McClellan has the diarrhea. What shall I do? The bottom is out of the tub, the bottom is out of the tub!" Meigs told him to "fix the bottom back in the tub" and rally the armies.

Lincoln again needed someone to reorganize and rejuvenate the Union armies, if only to protect Washington, which was vulnerable once more. For that task, no one was better than McClellan, so the president restored him to active command of all the forces in Washington. It was a controversial decision that was unpopular with his Cabinet, and Lincoln himself had been reluctant to do it. To Attorney General Edward Bates, the president "seemed wrung by the bitterest anguish—said he felt almost ready to hang himself."

Lee began marching north, and on September 5, Confederate forces, singing "Maryland, My Maryland," waded across the Potomac River, invaded the border state and quickly occupied the city of Frederick. On September 7, McClellan and his Army of the Potomac plodded out of the capital city in pursuit of Lee. "Please do not let him get off without being hurt," Lincoln pleaded to his general in a telegram.

Narrative resumes on page 72

ANTIETAM SIGNAL STATION
After the battle of Antietam, the Army of the Potomac Signal Corps built this signal station at the summit of a 1,058-foot mountain just east of Sharpsburg, Maryland, known locally as Red Hill. The perch provided a panoramic view of the battlefield. *(Library of Congress)*

THE DEAD OF ANTIETAM

In the wake of the Battle of Antietam, Alexander Gardner, the manager of
Mathew Brady's Washington gallery, photographed American dead on a field
of war for the first time. The gruesome photographs stunned New Yorkers,
who flocked to Brady's Broadway gallery to see "The Dead of Antietam"
photo exhibition a month after the battle. A *New York Times* story from
October 20, 1862, said: "Mr. Brady has done something to bring home to us the
terrible reality and earnestness of war. If he has not brought bodies and laid
them in our dooryard and along the streets, he has done something very like it."
Gardner took at least twenty different images of the dead at Antietam—all of
them in 3-D.

LONE GRAVE
The lone grave of a Union soldier sits under
a scraggly tree on the Antietam battlefield.
(Library of Congress)

1862
AND THE BATTLE OF
ANTIETAM

Chapter 03

BLOODY LANE (TOP)

A burial party works at a sunken road on the Antietam battlefield that was occupied by Confederate troops and became known as "Bloody Lane." *(Library of Congress)*

DUNKER CHURCH (BOTTOM)

Dead Confederate artillerymen are scattered around their limber near the Dunker Church. *(Bob Zeller Collection)*

HAGERSTOWN PIKE (OPPOSITE PAGE)

Confederates from Louisiana were photographed as they fell along the Hagerstown Pike on the Antietam battlefield. *(Library of Congress)*

A CONTRAST

The body of a young Confederate lies next to
the grave of a Union lieutenant from Michigan.
(Library of Congress)

Chapter **03**

GEN. McCLELLAN AND HIS WIFE (TOP)

A veteran of the Mexican War, George B. McClellan had left the army and was chief engineer of the Illinois Central Railroad when the Civil War started. While commanding the Union Army of the Potomac in 1861 and 1862, he forged a legacy as a skillful organizer but timid field commander. Here he poses with his wife, Ellen, at Mathew Brady's photographic gallery in Washington. *(Library of Congress)*

ROBERT E. LEE (BOTTOM)

Unwilling to fight against the South, Robert E. Lee resigned his U.S. Army commission the day after Virginia seceded from the Union and joined that state's forces as a major general. Shown here in a postwar Mathew Brady studio portrait, Lee took command of the Confederate Army of Northern Virginia in June 1862. No wartime 3-D photos of Lee are known to exist. *(Library of Congress)*

LINCOLN AND McCLELLAN (OPPOSITE PAGE)

Lincoln's liberal patience with his haughty commander had been worn thin when this image was taken as he met with McClellan on the Antietam battlefield on October 3, 1862. More than two weeks had passed since the battle, and McClellan had not moved. *(Library of Congress)*

Narrative continued from page 62

The two forces ultimately concentrated outside the village of Sharpsburg, Maryland, near the Potomac. Once there, McClellan took an extra day perfecting his lines, which gave Lee's far-flung troops more time to gather. The Battle of Antietam on September 17, 1862, ended in a draw. Even so, it was the bloodiest day in American history, with 22,720 killed, wounded, or missing, all in a single day in about six square miles—an area about the size of Beverly Hills, California. Lee withdrew his battered army into Virginia while McClellan lingered on the battlefield, calling for more men and horses. Lincoln's frustration grew until, on October 1, without wiring ahead, he boarded a Baltimore & Ohio train to visit his commander in the field. Lincoln spent two nights at Antietam, conferring with the Union commanders, visiting the wounded, and urging McClellan to advance into Virginia. He also took a few moments to pose for group photographs taken by photographer Alexander Gardner, who had captured dramatic images of the Antietam dead in the days after the battle.

On October 4, in Frederick, on his way back to Washington, Lincoln had begged off making a speech to the gathered masses, stating that "every word is so closely noted that it will not do to make trivial ones. . . ." Yet he was already destined to be castigated for his personal behavior, not for misspoken words, but for listening to a song. Riding in the back of an ambulance during his Antietam visit, Lincoln had turned to his close friend and bodyguard Ward Hill Lamon and asked him to sing the "little sad song" that Lamon sang on occasion and Lincoln loved so. Lamon did as he was asked, but when the song made the mood even more somber, he sought to brighten spirits with a minstrel number. Soon the story spread that the president had indulged in laughter and merriment on a battlefield where the wounded still lay in their sick beds and the dead were barely cold in their graves. Deeply stung by the criticism, Lincoln prepared a statement of defense but never released it. "If I have not established character enough to give the lie to this charge, I can only say that I am mistaken in my own estimate of myself," he said.

COMMANDER IN THE FIELD
Lincoln towers above the Union officers around him in this photograph taken on October 3, 1862, during his visit to the Antietam battlefield. Gen. George McClellan stands fourth from the right. Lincoln's friend and bodyguard, Ward Hill Lamon, sits at left. *(Bob Zeller Collection)*

WASHINGTON

∾ AT WAR ∾

Chapter **04**

THE BATTLE OF ANTIETAM, though inconclusive, gave Abraham Lincoln enough political leverage to take his boldest step as president. In Washington on September 22, 1862, he issued the Emancipation Proclamation and struck a death blow against slavery in the South. He had been planning the action for two months but believed he needed something resembling battlefield success, if not an outright victory, to give the proclamation sufficient credibility.

WHITE HOUSE CONSERVATORY

A Mathew Brady photographer took this stereo photograph in the White House conservatory, with Lincoln's personal secretary, John Nicolay, sitting at right. On the left is Sen. James W. Nesmith, a trusted adviser of Lincoln who represented Oregon and was in the Senate from 1861 to 1867. *(John J. Richter Collection)*

Although the proclamation is widely misconstrued as being the document that freed the slaves, emancipation was not that simple. Going on the assumption that the North would win the war, Lincoln gave the slave-holding states of the Confederacy until January 1, 1863, to return to the Union; if they did, slave owners could expect to either keep their slaves or be compensated for having to free them. In those states that remained in rebellion, however, all slaves would be considered free, at least by the Union, as of that day. And in most parts of the Confederacy that were under Union control, such as Beaufort, South Carolina, slaves were, in fact, free on the first day of 1863, with no compensation to the owners. Notably, the proclamation did not free the slaves of border states, although it created the legal framework for their eventual freedom. Even as the Confederacy condemned the proclamation and ignored its pronouncements, Lincoln's bold action reverberated far beyond the terms proscribed in the document. The Emancipation Proclamation brought the cause of the war—slavery—into sharp focus. Now Northern

and Southern parents alike knew their brave sons would shed blood to settle the issue once and for all; if the South lost, slavery was dead.

At the White House two days later, a band played patriotic music and a large crowd serenaded the president, who told them, "What I did, I did after very full deliberation, and under a very heavy and solemn sense of responsibility. I can only trust in God I have made no mistake."

It was common during the war for residents to serenade the president or pour into the streets in celebration of a political event or battlefield victory. From the moment the District of Columbia was created on July 16, 1790, by an act of Congress, Washington's number one business was politics.

Washington was then, as it is now, a city of people from other places. It grew slowly during its first seventy years and was a sleepy, Southern town at the beginning of the war. Buying and selling slaves was banned in 1850, but one could still own them in the district, and more than 3,100 of the city's 75,000 residents in 1860 were bondsmen. To satisfy Southern sensibilities, strict laws were designed to keep blacks—both free and slave—in their place. The police spent much of their time chasing down runaways and returning them to their masters. Slaves could be jailed for wandering too far from home or staying out past 10 P.M. They could be lashed with the whip for setting off firecrackers near a home or simply flying a kite within the city limits. With the advent of the war, though, slaves by the hundreds fled Virginia, took refuge in the city, and were welcomed into the war effort as laborers, servants—and eventually soldiers.

To the visitor, Washington had an unfinished appearance. Most of the broad, diagonal thoroughfares of Pierre-Charles L'Enfant's original street plan were still, like the country itself, avenues of sanguine promise and future growth. "As in 1800 and 1850, so in 1860, the same rude colony was camped in the same forest, with the same unfinished Greek temples for workrooms, and sloughs for roads," wrote Henry Adams, whose grandfather and great-grandfather had lived there as presidents. The unfinished Capitol building; the stump of the Washington monument, where work had stopped in 1854; the putrid Tiber Canal flanking the largely undeveloped Mall; the few public buildings, imposing but widely dispersed—all conspired to give the capital city its incomplete look.

"Its public buildings are splendid, its private buildings generally squalid," the *Atlantic Monthly* reported in 1861. "The houses are low, the rents high. The streets are broad, the crossings narrow. The hacks are black and the horses are white; the squares are triangular, except that of the Capitol, which is oval; and the water is so soft that it is hard to drink it even with the admixture of alcohol."

And there was plenty of alcohol to go around. The city's transient population, away from home for months on end, sought

PENNSYLVANIA AVENUE
In Washington, DC, the flag of the Union flutters over Pennsylvania Avenue on a breezy day in 1864 or 1865 in this E. & H. T. Anthony & Company photograph. Taken from a window of the Metropolitan Hotel, the image captures the recently finished Capitol in the distance. *(John J. Richter Collection)*

alternative comforts by liberally dipping in its trough of sinful pleasures. Wartime Washington had at least eighty-five bawdy houses where more than 420 prostitutes offered their services. There were so many establishments that the Military Provost Office monitored them and even developed a rating system.

The White House itself was worn-looking and drafty, with a front door key that dated to the Jefferson administration. When the Lincoln family arrived in 1861, they found threadbare carpets, dingy wallpaper, and, as one visitor observed, a mansion that had the look of "an old and unsuccessful hotel." Mary Lincoln immediately embarked on a program to refurbish the thirty-one-room mansion, but far exceeded her budget, earning the wrath of her husband, who knew that the overspending would not sit well with a country at war. But the biggest problem with the house was its location in the lowlands next to the Potomac River.

TWENTY-SIX MONTHS IN OFFICE (THIS PAGE)
Lincoln stands up for the camera for the first time as president in an image taken by photographer Thomas Le Mere at Mathew Brady's gallery on or about April 17, 1863. When Le Mere told the towering Lincoln that demand existed for a full-length standing photo, Lincoln replied in jest, "Can it be taken with a single negative?" *(Courtesy of the Center for Civil War Photography)*

CHECKING FERRY PASSES (OPPOSITE PAGE)
Union military guards check passes at the Mason's (now Roosevelt) Island landing of the ferry to Georgetown, which looms on the far side of the Potomac River. *(Library of Congress)*

The area smelled so rotten that Lincoln's secretary, John Hay, said, "The ghosts of twenty thousand drowned cats come in nights through the south windows." Willie Lincoln's fatal fever is often attributed to the unsanitary conditions around the White House and the fact that its water supply came from the Potomac River.

Unfinished or not, Washington was still the seat of power in the North, and the sleepy town with Southern style would become a city of vast military might. Its location at the very border of the Confederacy only served to intensify its role in the conflict. Washington would start the war all but undefended, and in those first two years it would become vulnerable, or at least feel vulnerable, time and time again. Only once would the city come under direct attack from the Confederates, though, and when that happened in 1864, Lincoln himself would be there to greet them.

WASHINGTON PANORAMA (TOP & OPPOSITE)
The Washington that Lincoln knew was extensively photographed in 3-D. In this pair of E. & H. T. Anthony & Company views, the camera is perched high in the Smithsonian Castle, looking northwest. The putrid Tiber Canal stretches across the scene, while behind it, on the right, sits the expansive Treasury Building. The top of the White House is visible above the distant trees. *(Robin Stanford Collection)*

THE SOUTH LAWN (BOTTOM)
This Anthony view, probably taken in 1861, includes a rare glimpse of a platoon of Union soldiers on the South Lawn of the White House. *(Robin Stanford Collection)*

WASHINGTON
AT WAR

Chapter 04

THE LINCOLN WHITE HOUSE
This was the White House when the room known
as the Lincoln bedroom was Abraham Lincoln's
office. We peer through the gates of Lafayette
Park to see the north façade of the mansion.
(John J. Richter Collection)

HANNIBAL HAMLIN
Vice President Hannibal Hamlin, served 1861–1864.
(Library of Congress)

WASHINGTON
AT WAR

Chapter 04

EDWARD BATES
Attorney General Edward Bates, served 1861–1864.
(Library of Congress)

AT WAR

Chapter 04

SALMON P. CHASE

Secretary of the Treasury Salmon P. Chase, served 1861–1864. *(Library of Congress)*

AT WAR

Chapter 04

KATE CHASE

Kate Chase, Salmon P. Chase's daughter, was
the leading belle of Washington politics while
her father was Secretary of the Treasury. Born
in 1840, she was in her early twenties when
she posed for this Mathew Brady portrait. Her
father was a widower, and she was considered
the first lady of the Cabinet. Her November 1863
marriage to Rhode Island senator and one-time
governor William Sprague was one of the biggest
Washington social events of the war. (*Library of
Congress*)

MONTGOMERY BLAIR

Postmaster General Montgomery Blair, served
1861–1864. *(Library of Congress)*

WASHINGTON
AT WAR

Chapter 04

GIDEON WELLES
Secretary of the Navy Gideon Welles, served
1861–1869. *(Library of Congress)*

SIMON CAMERON
Secretary of War Simon Cameron, served in 1861.
(Library of Congress)

AT WAR

Chapter 04

EDWIN M. STANTON

Secretary of War Edwin M. Stanton,
served 1861–1868. *(Library of Congress)*

WILLARD HOTEL (TOP)
Lincoln made the popular and prestigious Willard Hotel on Pennsylvania Avenue his headquarters in the days before he was inaugurated as president. *(John J. Richter Collection)*

GARDNER'S GALLERY (BOTTOM)
Photographer Alexander Gardner took some of Lincoln's best-known portraits here at his Washington gallery at Seventh and D Streets. Gardner, who took more photographs (thirty-three) of Lincoln than any other photographer, opened his gallery in May 1863 after leaving the employment of Mathew Brady. *(Courtesy Nelson-Atkins Museum of Art)*

THE WAR DEPARTMENT (OPPOSITE PAGE)
The War Department was next to the White House. During great battles, Lincoln haunted the telegraph room to see the latest dispatches from the front as they clicked in. *(John J. Richter Collection)*

MAJESTIC MANSION (TOP)

This view of the White House from the South Lawn shows on the left the conservatory, or greenhouse, where John Nicolay and native Americans posed for Brady's stereo camera. This photo was taken before the greenhouse burned in 1867 and was replaced with a larger structure. *(John J. Richter Collection)*

U.S. CAPITOL (BOTTOM)

The U.S. Capitol was expanded and its new dome was added during the Civil War. This image of the nearly completed building was taken in April 1865, when it was draped with mourning bunting in the wake of Lincoln's assassination. *(John J. Richter Collection)*

NATIVE AMERICANS AT THE WHITE HOUSE (OPPOSITE PAGE)

On March 27, 1863, Lincoln took time away from managing the war to greet a delegation of Cheyenne and Kiowa Indians on an official state visit to Washington, DC. Although Lincoln himself wasn't present, a Mathew Brady photographer posed the group in the White House conservatory. The woman standing at the far right closely resembles Mary Todd Lincoln, but the positive identification remains uncertain. Within twenty months, all four of the Indian leaders seated in the front would be dead. *(Michael Griffith Collection)*

GETTYSBURG

Chapter **05**

ON NOVEMBER 7, 1862, President Lincoln finally shed himself of the recalcitrant Gen. McClellan, who went home to Trenton, New Jersey, to await further orders, which never came. Lincoln's new commander, Gen. Ambrose Burnside, marched the Army of the Potomac to Fredericksburg, where he crossed the Rappahannock River and assaulted Gen. Lee's men as they waited behind a stone wall on the heights beyond the city. Almost thirteen thousand Union men fell, and their cries of agony echoed all the way back to Washington, gruesomely amplified when the ambulance wagons began arriving.

LITTLE ROUND TOP
About two weeks after the Battle of Gettysburg, Mathew Brady captured this expansive view from the summit of Little Round Top, a landmark of day two of the Battle of Gettysburg. This view looks north toward Cemetery Ridge. *(Library of Congress)*

In the U.S. Senate, angry Republican legislators looked for someone to blame, and found a scapegoat in Secretary of State William Seward, who submitted his resignation. Lincoln, however, declined to accept it and brought the warring factions together at the White House, skillfully quelling the revolt. "They wish to get rid of *me*, and I am sometimes half disposed to gratify them," Lincoln said. The political storm was just one more manifestation of a war going badly. The Christmas season was gloomy in Washington, now a city full of hospitals and suffering, and Lincoln sought to distract himself from the melancholy times by focusing on the execution of the Emancipation Proclamation when it went into effect on New Year's Day.

Lincoln replaced Burnside with Gen. Joseph Hooker, who led the Army of the Potomac to another massive disaster in the Battle of Chancellorsville in the spring of 1863. "Never, as long as I knew him, did {Lincoln} seem to be so broken up, so dispirited, and so ghostlike" than after the defeat, wrote journalist Noah Brooks, a close friend of the president. "Clasping his hands behind his back, he walked up and down the room, saying, 'My God! My God! What will the country say! What will the country say!'"

The news was better from the western front, where the decisive and aggressive Gen. Ulysses S. Grant was closing in on Vicksburg, intent on prying the Mississippi River from Confederate control. In Tennessee the year before, Grant had captured two key river bastions, Fort Henry and Fort Donelson, and driven the Rebels back in the bloody Battle of Shiloh. Lincoln longed for someone like Grant to lead the campaigns in the east.

Emboldened by his dramatic Chancellorsville victory—one that would be studied the world over by military strategists—Lee invaded the North once more, and by June 27, 1863, Confederate soldiers were advancing on Harrisburg, the Pennsylvania capital. Lincoln replaced Hooker with Gen. George G. Meade, who immediately led the Army of the Potomac across the Mason-Dixon Line in pursuit of Lee. The armies collided at Gettysburg, Pennsylvania, and fought there for three momentous days. When the guns finally fell silent, the Confederate army was in shreds, limping back to Virginia, ripe for a final, mortal blow.

Lincoln haunted the War Department telegraph office for the latest telegrams from the front, as he always did on the eve of major battles, and more good news arrived while he was there on July 7. The president quickly telegraphed the general-in-chief, Henry Halleck:

We have certain information that Vicksburg surrendered to General Grant on the 4th of July. Now, if General Meade can complete his work,

so gloriously prosecuted thus far, by the literal or substantial destruction of Lee's army, the rebellion will be over.

Lincoln was gratified by the victory at Gettysburg, but behind closed doors, he was furious with Meade for failing to deliver the finishing blow. "Our army held the war in the hollow of their hand, and they would not close it," Lincoln complained. To Meade, he wrote a blistering letter: "My dear general, I do not believe you appreciate the magnitude of the misfortune involved in Lee's escape. Your golden opportunity is gone, and I am distressed immeasurably because of it." Lincoln, upon further reflection, never sent the letter. Meade, after all, had taken command only days before the battle and his army had suffered its own terrible losses.

Lincoln also wrote to Grant, but he went ahead and sent this note, thanking the general for the capture of Vicksburg. Grant had a reputation for excessive drinking, and word got out that if the president could only find out what brand of whiskey the general liked, he would send "every general in the field a barrel of it." Lincoln disavowed the story but said laughing, "That would have been very good if I *had* said it. . . ."

Narrative resumes on page 114

WITH FIRM RESOLVE
Lincoln strikes a determined pose for the camera of government photographer Lewis Walker in this image taken sometime in 1863. *(Courtesy of the Center for Civil War Photography)*

SLAUGHTER PEN (TOP)

Now on his own, and striving to repeat his photographic coup at Antietam, Alexander Gardner hurried to Gettysburg with two associates and arrived two days after Pickett's Charge, while some of the dead soldiers were still on the field. He named this place at the base of Big Round Top "The Slaughter Pen." *(Library of Congress)*

HARVEST OF DEATH (BOTTOM)

Gardner and his associates, photographers James Gibson and Timothy O'Sullivan, took several images, including this one of a group of dead Union Soldiers, labeling the scene "A Harvest of Death." *(Library of Congress)*

THE ROSE FARM (OPPOSITE PAGE)

Gardner sold fifty-two different stereo views of Gettysburg; more than half showed human carnage. This view of Confederate dead on the southern part of the battlefield at the Rose Farm shows Gardner's photographic darkroom field wagon. *(Library of Congress)*

CULP'S HILL (TOP)

Mathew Brady and Alexander Gardner complemented each other with their photographic coverage at Gettysburg. Brady photographed areas that Gardner missed or overlooked, such as Culp's Hill and its battle-scarred trees. *(Library of Congress)*

MEADE IN THE FIELD (BOTTOM)

Lincoln appointed Gen. George G. Meade (standing just to the left of the door opening in this image taken at Brandy Station) commander of the Army of the Potomac on June 27, 1862, just four days before the Battle of Gettysburg started. *(Library of Congress)*

LUTHERAN THEOLOGICAL SEMINARY (OPPOSITE PAGE)

While Gardner's images were often gritty tableaus of death, Brady's photographs were more elegant, with attractive, well-composed landscapes and inspiring portraits. This is the Lutheran Theological Seminary, where Union Gen. John Buford stood in the cupola and watched thousands of Confederates advance on his outnumbered cavalrymen to begin the Battle of Gettysburg. *(Library of Congress)*

Chapter **05**

MEADE'S HEADQUARTERS (TOP)

In this small farmhouse on Cemetery Ridge, Meade and his generals gathered on the evening of the second day's battle and decided to stay put and fight on. Pickett's Charge came the following day. *(Library of Congress)*

EVERGREEN CEMETERY GATEHOUSE (BOTTOM)

The Evergreen Cemetery Gatehouse was the only prominent feature on the Gettysburg battlefield photographed by both Gardner and Brady, this being the Brady view. Some of the gatehouse windows were shattered during the battle. *(Library of Congress)*

Chapter 05

JOHN BURNS

Brady photgraphed citizen-hero John Burns,
a former town constable, who put on his high-
crowned felt hat, took up his flint-lock musket
and powder horn, and marched out to the
battlefield on the first day. The sixty-nine-year-
old Burns was seriously wounded in the leg and
achieved national fame. *(Library of Congress)*

THREE REBS

In Brady's most famous stereo photograph from Gettysburg, three Confederate prisoners pose on Seminary Ridge next to fence rails and beams that were used by the Southerners as makeshift breastworks. The town of Gettysburg is in the background. *(John J. Richter Collection)*

WITH GLASSES AND A NEWSPAPER

On August 9, 1863, about five weeks after the battle of Gettysburg, Lincoln paid his first visit to Gardner's Gallery in Washington, sitting for five photos and standing for one. Although he maintained a presidential countenance in each view, "he was in very good spirits" wrote his secretary, John Hay. *(Library of Congress)*

LINCOLN ARRIVING FOR THE GETTYSBURG ADDRESS

As President Lincoln arrived for the consecration of the Soldiers' National Cemetery at Gettysburg on November 19, 1863, Alexander Gardner took two stereoscopic images within about sixty seconds of each other. Each photo and its detail appear back to back on the next four pages. In each image, while kids mug for the camera in the foreground, Lincoln can be seen arriving for the ceremony on horseback, with his distinctive, bearded profile and top hat rising above the crowd. One day, hopefully, someone will find incontrovertible evidence that Gardner was working fast to photograph the arriving president as opposed to taking two commonplace images of the crowd. In the meantime, the key elements deep within these photos—the top hat and beard, the distinctive Lincoln profile, the white riding gloves, the lack of a marshal's sash, the proximity of the eagle-topped pole, the corridor of troops he appears to be riding in, the attention directed his way—all point to Lincoln's presence. Gardner must have been disappointed that Lincoln was minuscule in the images. Although the negatives survived, no original Gardner's Gallery stereo view cards of these images are known to exist, suggesting that he printed few, if any, for public sale.

Evergreen
Gatehouse
↓

LINCOLN
↓

Speakers'
Platform
↓

Tent For
Edward Everett
↓

GETTYSBURG

FIRST PHOTO OF ARRIVAL & DETAIL

As he took the first stereograph of Lincoln arriving, photographer Alexander Gardner may have been less than delighted that the photographic platform that allowed him to shoot above the crowd was so far removed from the action, with so much open space between him and the rear of the throng, as well as the president. Lincoln's presence in the photographs became apparent when John J. Richter viewed high-resolution scans of the images in their original 3-D format in 2007. Only after examining the scene in depth and high-res detail could Richter see Lincoln's distinctive profile and top hat sticking above the crowd. Most of the military men are looking toward Lincoln, not toward the speaker's stand to the right of him. *(Library of Congress; detail by John J. Richter)*

Chapter 05

SECOND PHOTO OF ARRIVAL & DETAIL

In Gardner's second image, taken moments after the first, Lincoln has barely moved. His back is toward the speaker's stand, apparently because he turned to face the lined troops head-on. In the mid-foreground of the full image, the young boy with the light pants cuffs strikes a formal pose in nearly the same spot he stood for the first image. Lincoln was wearing white riding gloves during the procession to the cemetery, and the detail shows the president raising his white-gloved left hand and arm, which are blurred because he moved them during the several seconds it took to expose the photo. The tent was erected for the primary speaker, Edward Everett, because he planned to speak for two hours and frequently needed a restroom. *(Library of Congress; detail by John J. Richter)*

Evergreen
Gatehouse
↓

LINCOLN
↓

Speakers'
Platform
↓

Tent For
Edward Everett
↓

Narrative continued from page 98

In Gettysburg, a bloody summer gave way to fall, and local attorney David Wills invited the president to speak at the dedication of the cemetery the town had created for the Union soldiers who perished there. Lincoln made an exception to his general rule of declining the countless speech invitations he received and agreed to appear in Gettysburg, where he planned to keep his remarks "short, short, short" after the oration of Edward Everett, the noted Massachusetts politician. Everett spoke for almost two hours, recounting the battle in detail. Lincoln spoke for two minutes, but the ten sentences of his Gettysburg Address make up one of the most memorable speeches in mankind's history.

Four score and seven years ago our fathers brought forth on this continent a new nation, conceived in Liberty, and dedicated to the proposition that all men are created equal.

Now we are engaged in a great civil war, testing whether that nation, or any nation, so conceived and so dedicated, can long endure. We are met on a great battlefield of that war. We have come to dedicate a portion of that field, as a final resting place for those who here gave their lives that that nation might live. It is altogether fitting and proper that we should do this.

But, in a larger sense, we can not dedicate—we can not consecrate —we can not hallow this ground. The brave men, living and dead, who struggled here, have consecrated it, far above our poor power to add or detract. The world will little note, nor long remember, what we say here, but it can never forget what they did here. It is for us the living, rather, to be dedicated here to the unfinished work which they who fought here have thus far so nobly advanced. It is rather for us to be here dedicated to the great task remaining before us—that from these honored dead we take increased devotion to that cause for which they gave the last full measure of devotion—that we here highly resolve that these dead shall not have died in vain—that this nation, under God, shall have a new birth of freedom—and that government of the people, by the people, for the people, shall not perish from the earth.

Initially the speech received mixed reviews. The Democratic *Chicago Times* mocked the "silly, flat and dishwatery utterances." But Everett, who had shared the stage that day, recognized its greatness. He wrote Lincoln: "I should be glad if I could flatter myself that I came as near to the central idea of the occasion, in two hours, as you did in two minutes."

AFTER THE CEREMONY BEGAN
Gardner took a third stereo view after the ceremony got underway. Although not identifiable here, Lincoln is somewhere close to the large banner that has been unfurled at the center of the speaker's stand. In the foreground, arms are stacked and some soldiers are sitting on the ground. *(Library of Congress)*

LINCOLN

~ AND HIS FAMILY ~

Chapter 06

IN A WAR that hurled brother against brother, the White House itself was home to a family pulled by heartstrings attached to both North and South. Mary Lincoln's half-sister, Emilie, had married Kentucky native and West Point graduate Benjamin Hardin Helm in 1856. Helm was a staunch Southern Democrat, but he and Emilie had been houseguests of the Lincolns in Springfield, and the brothers-in-law had become warm friends.

Two weeks after the clash at Fort Sumter, Lincoln offered to commission Helm as a Union army major and proposed to name him paymaster. Helm agonized and lost sleep over the offer—"generous beyond anything I have ever known"—but ultimately

HUMBLE ORIGINS
The Kentucky log cabin in which Lincoln was born in 1809 was taken apart before Lincoln's death. This 1894 reproduction was built to approximate the original cabin. *(John J. Richter Collection)*

declined it. Instead he became a colonel in the Confederate cavalry and was soon promoted to brigadier general.

Mary Ann Todd Lincoln had Southern blood and had grown up in a Kentucky mansion tended to by house servants. As a child, Mary's "mammy" was a slave named Sally, one of several owned by her influential father, Robert Smith Todd, a wealthy Lexington banker and Whig politician. State and national leaders, including Henry Clay, frequently stayed with the Todds while in Lexington, and Mary came to love the spirited political discussions and aura of power and influence borne by their distinguished houseguests. After attending a fashionable women's academy to age seventeen, Mary Todd moved to Springfield, Illinois, to live with her sister and brother-in-law, Elizabeth and Ninian Edwards.

Abraham Lincoln could not have been more different from his wife-to-be. He was a child of the frontier, born in a one-room log cabin in Kentucky in 1809. Later, when he was running for president, his supporters would use the rough-hewn "railsplitter" persona to emphasize Lincoln's ruggedness and pioneering spirit, but for many years he did all he could to distance himself from his backwoods roots.

When Lincoln was seven, his father moved the family about 130 miles west to the free state of Indiana, and later on to Illinois, where a towering, rail-thin but strong twenty-two-year-old set out on his own in 1831 as "a friendless, uneducated, penniless boy—working on a flat boat at 10 dollars per month." Lincoln received only about a year of formal schooling, but he hungered for knowledge and educated himself. Captivated by politics, he nonetheless lost his first political campaign in 1832 for the Illinois General Assembly at age twenty-three. Five years later, after teaching himself law and passing the bar examination, Lincoln moved to Springfield and hung out his shingle as an attorney. There, in 1839, he met Mary Todd at a cotillion.

Mary was attracted to Abraham, even though he was several rungs lower on the social ladder. He was rough, yes, but as an attorney and politician, he was keenly ambitious. As a companion, he was witty, kind, and attentive. Mary shared his love for politics, and they were of a like mind on most issues. Their courtship, though, was rocky. When Lincoln first proposed, Mary accepted, but the Todd family vehemently opposed the marriage, believing him unworthy of their daughter. He called off the engagement for a time, but their mutual

VIEW FROM THE WHITE HOUSE
This early postwar view shows the scene Lincoln saw, including the unfinished Washington Monument, from the south portico of the White House.
(Michael Griffith Collection)

attraction persisted, and they were finally married in 1842. The first of their four sons, Robert, was born the following year.

Abraham and Mary were devoted to each other and, by all accounts, enjoyed a stable marriage despite her temper and radical mood swings. Lincoln doted on his wife, tending to her many needs like a handmaiden to a diva. The lasting effects of Edward's death were mitigated by her pregnancy with Willie, but she was never quite the same after Willie died in 1862. She had periodic migraine headaches that seemed to worsen after a head injury she suffered in a carriage accident in Washington on July 2, 1863—the second day of the Battle of Gettysburg.

While the Lincolns were in Washington, the happiest times for the family came at the thirty-four-room "cottage" they used on the grounds of Soldier's Home, a facility for invalid veterans in a wooded, hilly area about four miles north of the White House. They began going there in June 1862 as a way to escape the heat of the lower city, the lack of privacy at the White House, and the oppressive sadness of Willie's death. In mid-June or early July, White House staff would load furniture, clothing, and other possessions onto as many as nineteen wagons and head up Vermont Avenue and Seventh Street Road to Soldier's Home. At the cottage, Lincoln could escape the endless obligations of the presidency and play with Tad or read Shakespeare. But he frequently brought work with him or met with cabinet members, often with Secretary of War Edwin Stanton, who also had a small "summer home" at Soldier's Home. They spent three long summers at the Soldier's Home cottage, with Lincoln commuting back and forth to the White House each day by horseback or wagon, until the family's annual return to the White House in early November.

In late September 1863, while Mary and Tad were visiting New York, the War Department telegraph clicked out the news of the Union defeat at Chickamauga, along the Georgia-Tennessee border. And with this news came word of the death of Confederate Gen. Ben Helm. Later that fall, Helm's widow, Emilie, Mary's half-sister, sought to leave the Deep South and return home to Kentucky, which had remained in the Union. Lincoln issued a pass authorizing the move, but when she was detained at Fort Monroe, he had her brought directly to the White House, where she was greeted with all the warmth due a beloved relative. Another of Mary's half-sisters, Martha Todd White, also received Lincoln's permission to come to Washington (though not to the White House). Once there, however, she flaunted her Confederate sympathies and became such a problem that the president gave her a choice: leave immediately or be jailed in the Old Capitol Prison. Lincoln's animosity toward Martha did not extend to Emilie, though, and for that week in December 1863, she reunited with Mary, and they shared the grief of their losses, and talked of the old days, even as both remained staunchly loyal to their opposing causes. "Oh, Emilie," Mary said, "will we ever awake from this hideous nightmare?"

SURVEYING EQUIPMENT

Lincoln used this surveying equipment as deputy surveyor of Sangamon County, Illinois, from 1833 to 1836. Surveying was one of many odd jobs he had before becoming a lawyer. The powder horn reportedly was carried by Lincoln's grandfather during the Revolutionary War. *(John J. Richter Collection)*

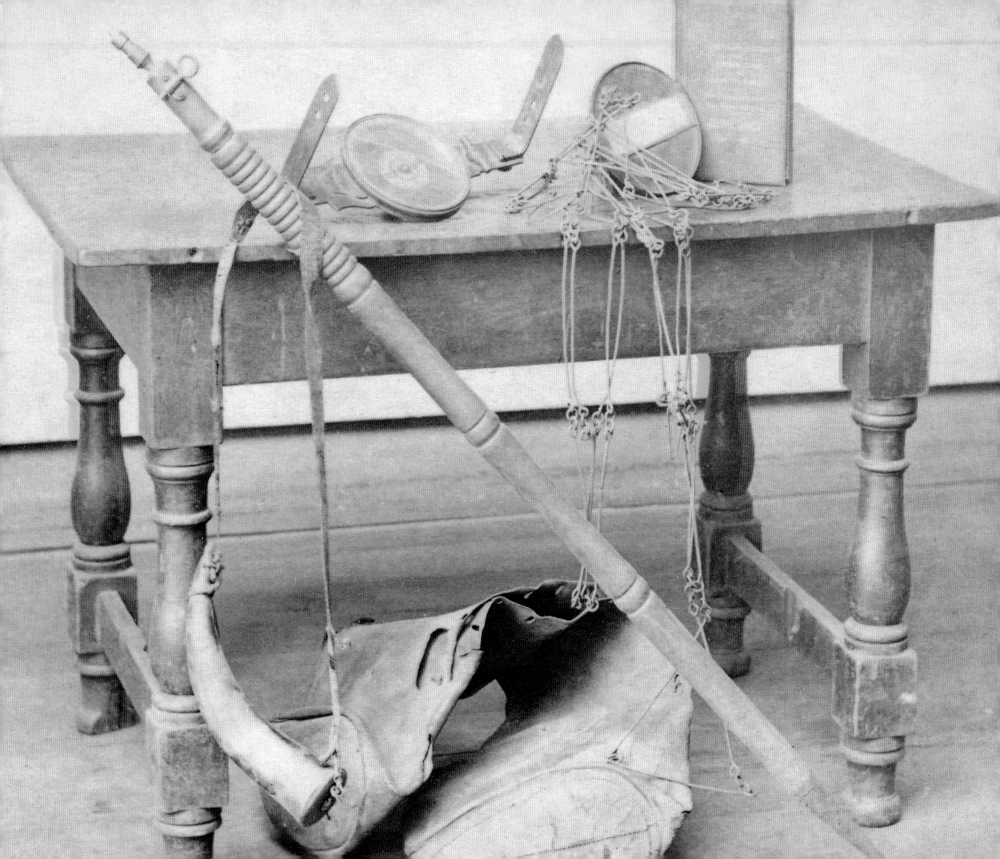

AFTER THE GETTYSBURG ADDRESS

On January 8, 1864, Lincoln sat for this portrait in the Congressional chair at Mathew Brady's studio in Washington. Among the known stereoscopic images of Lincoln, this one was taken closest to the time he gave the Gettysburg Address. *(Courtesy of the Center for Civil War Photography)*

AND HIS FAMILY

Chapter 06

MARY LINCOLN

Mary Todd Lincoln loved flowers and often posed
with them in her hair or hands, or in this case,
both. Although ill-tempered and emotionally
fragile, she was well-bred and stylish. *(Library
of Congress)*

AND HIS FAMILY

Chapter 06

HER INAUGURAL BALL DRESS
Mary Todd Lincoln, forty-three, was photographed
wearing her inaugural ball dress at Mathew Brady's
studio in 1861. *(Library of Congress)*

TAD LINCOLN

Thomas "Tad" Lincoln, born in 1853, was just
shy of eight years old when his father became
president. This circa 1861 photo shows him at
about that age. Wrote Lincoln's secretary, John
Hay, "Tad was a merry, warm-blooded, kindly little
boy, perfectly lawless, and full of odd fancies. . . ."
(John J. Richter Collection)

ROBERT LINCOLN

Robert was the oldest of the four Lincoln sons.
Born in 1843, he lived until 1926—the only Lincoln
child to reach full adulthood. This 1861 image
shows Robert at about eighteen years of age,
when he was a student at Harvard University.
(*Library of Congress*)

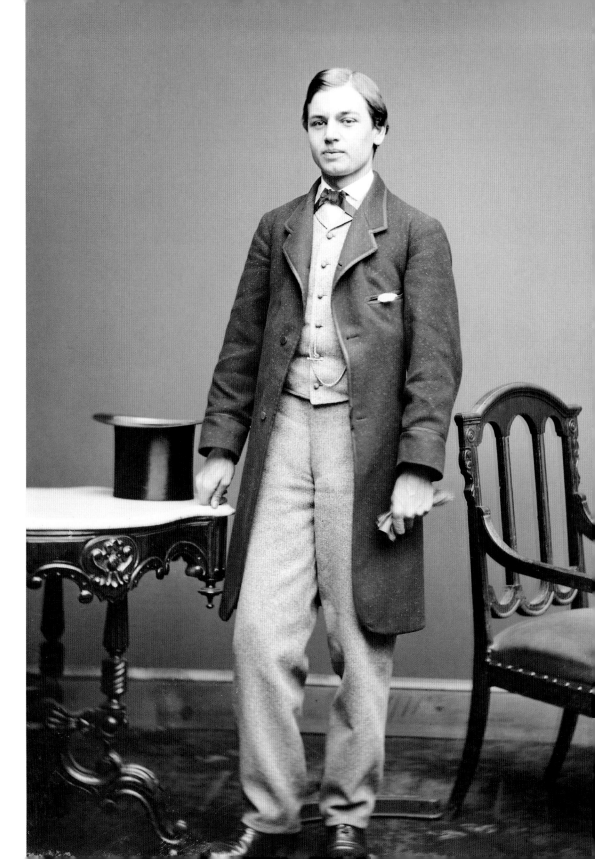

AND HIS FAMILY

Chapter 06

A DISTINGUISHED LIFE
Robert Lincoln served on Gen. Ulysses S. Grant's
staff, was secretary of war in the 1880s, became
president of the Pullman Company, and lived
long enough to personally attend the 1922
dedication of his father's memorial on the Mall
in Washington, DC. *(Library of Congress)*

AND HIS FAMILY

Chapter 06

SOLDIER'S HOME GUARDHOUSE (TOP)
Lincoln passed this guardhouse at Soldier's Home, in Washington, DC, many times on his way to his summer cottage. The sign on the gate says, "Visitors Are Not Permitted on Sunday." *(John J. Richter Collection)*

STANTON'S COTTAGE (BOTTOM)
Lincoln's fierce Secretary of War, Edwin Stanton, also maintained a "summer home" at the Soldier's Home, shown in this view. *(John J. Richter Collection)*

LINCOLN'S SUMMER HOME (OPPOSITE PAGE)
Although it was called a summer "cottage," this home within the grounds of Soldier's Home had thirty-four rooms. It provided a respite and a private haven from the all-too-public White House. *(John J. Richter Collection)*

LINCOLN
AND HIS FAMILY

Chapter 06

HAREWOOD HOSPITAL
Wounded Union soldiers on the mend sit on
their beds, with mosquito netting pulled back,
at Harewood Hospital, a military hospital near
Soldier's Home in Washington, DC. The Lincolns
likely visited convalescing soldiers here. (*Library
of Congress*)

HAREWOOD HOSPITAL MESS HALL
Alexander Gardner took this vivid 3-D view of
the Harewood Hospital mess hall, with its new
heaters, and tables set for the next meal. *(Library
of Congress)*

LANDSCAPING LINCOLN'S WHITE HOUSE
Landscapers dressed to the nines smooth the
gravel driveway in front of the south façade of the
Lincoln White House in this E. & H. T. Anthony &
Company stereo view. *(John Weiler Collection)*

1864
A YEAR OF
ALL-OUT WAR

Chapter 07

UNLIKE THE CHEERLESS holiday season of 1862, high spirits and optimism abounded in Washington during the Christmas season of 1863. "We seemed to have reached a new stage in the war," William Seward's son, Fred, wrote in a letter. "Gayety has become as epidemic in Washington this winter as gloom was last winter." In *Harper's Weekly*, artist Thomas Nast's depiction of New Year's Day showed a sketch of a Union soldier toasting his family next to one of a Confederate widow and her children, bereft of home and hope, kneeling at the grave of their husband and father. The tide had turned, victory seemed inevitable, and President Lincoln hoped to find a way to end the

BRADY AND BURNSIDE

Mathew Brady became Grant's official headquarters photographer in 1864 and visited the army at Cold Harbor in early June 1864. In this stereo view, Brady sits with Gen. Ambrose Burnside, who is reading a Washington newspaper. *(Library of Congress)*

war quickly. And for that job, he turned to his star in the west, Gen. Ulysses S. Grant.

On March 1, 1864, Lincoln nominated Grant to become lieutenant general, a field rank previously held only by George Washington, and made him commander of all of the Union armies. Grant slipped unnoticed into the capital city on March 8, but when word got out that he was in town, he was treated like a conquering hero. "Whatever happens, there will be no turning back," Grant said after the Army of the Potomac crossed the Rapidan River and moved south in early May. Here was a commander with the attitude Lincoln had been looking for.

But Grant's relentless pursuit came at a terrible cost. The dead piled up like never before, and the wounded strained the hospitals that now seemed to be everywhere in the city. More than seventeen thousand Union men fell in Grant's first battle with Robert E. Lee in the Wilderness; another seventeen thousand

were killed, wounded, or missing after two weeks of clashes at Spotsylvania. "The immense slaughter of our brave men chills and sickens us all," Secretary of the Navy Gideon Welles wrote in his diary on June 2. "The hospitals are crowded with the thousands of mutilated and dying heroes who have poured out their blood for the Union cause." The following day, at Cold Harbor, as many as seven thousand fell in a single, bloody hour. By the end of June, the Union could count more than sixty thousand new casualties. But no decisive victory appeared in sight.

Speaking in Philadelphia, Lincoln lamented that the war—"one of the most terrible"—had "carried mourning to almost every home, until it can almost be said that heavens are hung in black." But he was resolute. "We accepted this war for an object, a worthy object," he said, "and the war will end when that object is attained." The crowd—fathers and mothers, sons and daughters, widows and wounded veterans—erupted in cheers.

In July, Robert E. Lee sent Gen. Jubal Early back into Maryland to open another front and hopefully force Grant to react, relieving some of the stress in Virginia. Early brushed aside Union forces at the Monocacy River near Frederick and advanced toward Washington, entering the District of Columbia near its northern point. The land was still pastures and forests back then, and alongside the old Seventh Street Road leading toward downtown, the imposing ramparts of Fort Stevens, one of sixty-eight bastions that circled the city, provided a formidable obstacle for

WOUNDED AT FREDERICKSBURG
Wounded Union soldiers from the Battle of Spotsylvania rest on the grounds of the Marye House in Fredericksburg, Virginia, in the late spring of 1864. *(Library of Congress)*

would-be invaders. A mile and a half south was Soldier's Home and the president's summer cottage. The family was in residence but heeded the call to evacuate to the White House. Most of the Union's fresh troops were out fighting the war, and alarm spread through the city as local commanders stitched together a motley assemblage of invalid soldiers, convalescents, mechanics, cooks, teamsters, and civilians to protect the capital. A worried Lincoln encouraged Grant to personally come back, but Grant sent a corps of his army instead.

PAGE
140

1864
A YEAR OF

ALL-OUT WAR

Chapter 07

THE PENNY PROFILE (TOP)
A variant of this profile, taken by Anthony Berger at Brady's Washington gallery on February 9, 1864, was used to create the design on the Lincoln penny. *(Courtesy of the Center for Civil War Photography)*

BLACK INFANTRYMEN (BOTTOM)
Of the reported 178,895 African American soldiers in the Union army during the war, these two ended up in front of an E. & H. T. Anthony & Company camera at Dutch Gap, Virginia, in late 1864, posing with their muskets. *(Library of Congress)*

COUNCIL OF WAR (OPPOSITE PAGE)
Gen. Ulysses S. Grant, sitting in front of the twin trees, meets with his generals outside Massaponax Church in Spotsylvania County, Virginia, on May 21, 1864. The Union officers had removed church pews from the sanctuary to have a place to sit. *(Library of Congress)*

1864
A YEAR OF

Chapter **07**

HOUSE NEAR FT. STEVENS (THIS PAGE)

As Jubal Early's Confederates skirmished and demonstrated before Fort Stevens on July 11 and 12, 1864, shell fire damaged this nearby home. *(Library of Congress)*

WHAT LINCOLN SAW (OPPOSITE PAGE)

This is the landscape that Lincoln saw as he stood on the parapet of Fort Stevens in the District of Columbia, watching the action as the Confederates threatened the capital city. The camera in this E. & H. T. Anthony & Company view is in front of the fort, next to a destroyed dwelling, and faces north up the Seventh Street Road, the route used by the Confederates to enter the District of Columbia. *(Bob Zeller Collection)*

1864
A YEAR OF
ALL-OUT WAR

Chapter 07

On July 11, General Early organized his troops in front of Fort Stevens and began extensive skirmishing as Lincoln himself watched from the parapet, taking cover only after a stern warning from an officer. The following day, the skirmishing continued as Early feigned preparations for a full-scale assault. Lincoln again visited, again stood on the parapet while under fire, and once more was told to get down, this time after a Pennsylvania surgeon standing near him was struck down by sniper fire. At Fort Stevens, Lincoln became the first and only sitting president to come under enemy fire on a battlefield.

Lincoln faced a fierce battle on the political front as well. He tangled with leaders of his own party over terms of reconstruction and by August was hearing, and was himself convinced, that he would not be reelected. On August 23, he drafted a memo regarding the transition of power in the event of his loss, writing, "This morning, as for some days past, it seems exceedingly probable that this Administration will not be re-elected."

To run against Lincoln, the Democrats nominated George B. McClellan, with a platform that vowed to negotiate with the South and end the war peacefully. Even Lincoln's supporters were urging him to come to terms with the South. Two days after McClellan's nomination, however, just as Lincoln's political future seemed to reach its nadir, Gen. William Tecumseh Sherman, who had succeeded Grant in the west, captured the city of Atlanta. Instantly the political landscape changed, and Lincoln easily won reelection in November. Late-night serenaders came to the White House, and the president greeted them from a second-floor window, where he said, "It has demonstrated that a people's government can

sustain a national election, in the midst of a great civil war. Until now it has not been known to the world that this was a possibility. It shows also how *sound*, and how *strong* we still are."

A BATTLE FOR ATLANTA
General Sherman marched into Georgia and, during the battle for Atlanta on July 22, 1864, his guns demolished the mansion of the Ponder family. *(Library of Congress)*

1864
A YEAR OF

ALL-OUT WAR

Chapter 07

ULYSSES S. GRANT
Ulysses S. Grant, wearing a lieutenant
general's three stars in this studio portrait,
was a commander whose talent and strategy
"consisted in accumulating overwhelming
numbers," Gen. Robert E. Lee wrote his son
in 1864. But after Grant's generous surrender
terms, Lee reportedly said that his treatment
of the Confederate army was "without parallel
in the civilized world." *(Library of Congress)*

1864
A YEAR OF

ALL-OUT WAR

Chapter 07

ROBERT E. LEE

Gen. Robert E. Lee, shown here as a civilian after the war, was "a man of much dignity, with an impassible face," Ulysses S. Grant wrote in his memoirs. At the surrender, "it was impossible to say whether he felt inwardly glad that the end had finally come, or felt sad over the result, and was too manly to show it. Whatever his feelings, they were entirely concealed from my observation. . . ."
(Library of Congress)

WILLIAM TECUMSEH SHERMAN

When Lincoln summoned Gen. Grant east to go after Gen. Lee and his army, he replaced Grant in the west with Gen. William Tecumseh Sherman, one of the Union army's most capable and aggressive commanders. *(Library of Congress)*

A TOWERING PRESENCE
President Lincoln posed for this standing portrait
at photographer Mathew Brady's studio on
January 8, 1864. "When I get all the kinks out,
I am six feet four inches," Lincoln said.
(John J. Richter Collection)

A DISTANT ENEMY

This placid scene of African American Union soldiers in Fort Burnham (formerly the Confederate Fort Harrison) below Richmond, Virginia, is actually a rare glimpse of Yankees and Rebels facing off on a battlefront. The parapet of the new Confederate fort, with at least two soldiers atop it, looms at the upper left center of the photograph. *(Library of Congress)*

THE
FINAL MONTHS

Chapter **08**

ON THE NIGHT of December 15, 1864, an assistant awakened Lincoln. The president came to the second-floor landing at the White House dressed in his nightshirt, holding a flickering candle as he peered down the steps at the two men below him. What had happened?

Excitement stitched the faces of Secretary of War Edwin Stanton and Maj. Thomas Eckert from the telegraph office, who had rushed over from the War Department with two fresh telegrams from the west. Victory was imminent at Nashville, Stanton said. Union Gen. George Thomas, after exasperating Lincoln and Grant with his methodical battle preparations until they

FREE BLACKS IN RICHMOND
Slaves no more, a group of African Americans, young and old, posed for Alexander Gardner's stereo camera in Richmond, Virginia, on June 9, 1865. The gutted shell of the Gallego Mills towers behind the group. *(Library of Congress)*

were on the verge of firing him, had finally attacked and broken the Confederate line. A complete rout was all but certain.

More good news arrived on the evening of Christmas Day. A telegram arrived from Gen. William T. Sherman, whose army had been massed around Savannah, Georgia, for two weeks after slicing and burning through Georgia in the "March to the Sea." Sherman wrote to Lincoln: "I beg to present you as a Christmas gift the city of Savannah with 150 heavy guns & plenty of ammunition & also about 25,000 bales of cotton." The good news now was as frequent as the bad news of 1861 and 1862, and a relieved and grateful president responded to Sherman:

Many, many, thanks for your Christmas gift—the capture of Savannah. . . . And, taking the work of Gen. Thomas into the count, as it should be taken, it is indeed a great success . . . it brings those who sat in darkness, to see a great light. But what next? I suppose it will be safer if I leave Gen. Grant and yourself to decide.

Lincoln did just that and set his own sights on putting the final nail in the coffin of slavery. A new Constitutional amendment banning slavery throughout the United States had passed the Senate in 1864, but many Democrats opposed the measure, and it failed to gain the necessary two-thirds majority in the House. When Congress assembled on December 5, 1864, Lincoln asked that the amendment—the thirteenth—be reconsidered, and he threw his considerable political weight behind the drive to get it passed when debate began on January 6, 1865. For the rest of the month, Congress wrangled over the issue, and, on January 31, spectators filled the galleries to watch the dramatic House vote. The amendment passed by three votes.

Lincoln well understood the irony of the decision. Before his inauguration in 1861, Congress had passed an earlier thirteenth amendment—this one *protecting* slavery—but the war started before the measure could be ratified. As he had told civil rights pioneer Sojourner Truth in 1864, "If the people over the [Potomac] river had behaved themselves, I could not have done what I have."

In the first days of March 1865, citizens packed Washington's hotels, just as they had in 1861. As Lincoln prepared to take the oath of office for his second term as president, the country was close to a watershed moment in its history, just as it had been four years earlier. War clouds had gathered in 1861; now they were clearing. But those four years and all of their sorrows were etched in Lincoln's countenance. His face was lined, his eyes sunken and tired. He was, John Hay wrote, "in mind, body and nerves a very different man at the second inauguration from the one who had taken the oath in 1861. He continued always the same kindly, genial, and cordial spirit he had been at first; but the boisterous

laughter became less frequent year by year; the eye grew veiled by constant meditation on momentous subjects; the air of reserve and detachment from his surroundings increased."

Lincoln recognized the change in himself, telling Joshua Speed, his close friend, "Speed, I am a little alarmed about myself; just feel my hand." It was cold and clammy, Speed recalled, and his feet were, too, because they steamed when he put them close to the fire.

The city's population more than doubled during the war, and Washington became a vast military zone. Its hospitals treated more than twenty thousand convalescing soldiers. The urban landscape was now dotted with military warehouses, factories, supply depots, and administrative buildings. Many of the hundreds of soldiers who stood in crisp lines in front of the east face of the Capitol for Lincoln's second inauguration on

SECOND INAUGURATION (OPPOSITE)
In this first of two known stereographs of Lincoln's second inauguration, we get a less-than-sharp glimpse of the president seated to the left of the podium as the crowd begins to file in. *(Courtesy of the Center for Civil War Photography)*

INAUGURAL ADDRESS AND CROWD
(PAGES 156-157)
As Lincoln actually delivers his brief but memorable Second Inaugural Address, the crowd before him is orderly and attentive, save for a group of boisterous young men at lower right who are shouting and gesturing toward the podium. *(Library of Congress)*

March 4, 1865, were African American, and high above them, the Statue of Freedom stood atop a finished dome.

As at Gettysburg, Lincoln did not speak long. His second inaugural address—less than seven hundred words—offered hope and inspiration. A burst of sunlight broke through the clouds as he rose to speak, and the moment "made my heart jump," he said.

The final words of the address are among his greatest: *With malice toward none; with charity for all; with firmness in the right, as God gives us to see the right, let us strive on to finish the work we are in; to bind up the nation's wounds; to care for him who shall have borne the battle, and for his widow, and his orphan—to do all which may achieve and cherish a just, and a lasting peace, among ourselves, and with all nations.*

With the new term came new challenges, especially that of how to approach the reconstruction of the United States, with North and South united. The war was not quite over, but the outcome was assured, and Lincoln favored leniency, even to the point of allowing the Confederate soldiers to keep their arms. The more radical members of his Republican party, however, favored a much harsher, punitive approach.

The second term also brought the usual rush of office seekers and public visitors who once again filled the White House. After four years in the pressure cooker of the presidency, Lincoln sometimes failed to suffer fools gladly, and could unleash a sharp temper. When a Pennsylvania commoner wrote to remind him that "white men is in class number one and black men is in class number two and must be governed by white men forever,"

Lincoln was riled enough to respond, his words dripping with sarcasm. Lincoln asked the correspondent to tell him "whether you are either a white man or black one, because in either case, you can not be regarded as an entirely impartial judge. It may be that you belong to a third or fourth class of *yellow* or *red* men, in which case the impartiality of your judgment would be more apparent."

It seemed impossible for Lincoln to escape them, making his rare moments of relaxation all the more important. His favorite escape during his presidency, aside from unwinding at the Soldier's Home cottage, was to attend the theater. Lincoln went to shows at the three major Washington theaters at least thirty-two times during his presidency, mostly with Mary. They attended Grover's Theater seven different nights during a three-week span in February and March 1864 to watch Edwin Booth, the country's leading actor, star in *Richard III*, *Julius Caesar*, *The Merchant of Venice*, *Hamlet*, and other plays. They also went to Ford's Theatre, after it reopened in 1863 following a fire, to see John Wilkes Booth, Edwin's younger brother, perform in *The Marble Heart*.

On March 15, 1865, Lincoln went to Grover's Theater not so much to see *The Magic Flute*, but to escape the White House. One of the president's guests, Gen. James Grant Wilson, noticed that Lincoln looked weary and paid no attention to the play. When Wilson made light of it, Lincoln said, "I have not come for the

GRANT TAKES PETERSBURG
Dead Confederates lay in the trenches outside Petersburg the day after Union forces broke through Rebel lines on April 2, 1865. *(Library of Congress)*

play, but for the rest. I am hounded to death by office-seekers, who pursue me early and late, and it is simply to get two or three hours' relief that I am here." The president paused, concluding, "I wonder if we shall be tormented in heaven with them, as well as with bores and fools?" Then he closed his eyes.

ARTILLERY PARK (TOP)
A mortar and a heavy gun mounted on a disabled carriage are part of a vast artillery park at Broadway Landing on the Appomattox River near Petersburg in April 1865. *(Library of Congress)*

A CITY IN RUINS (BOTTOM)
When Lincoln came into Richmond, Virginia, on April 4, 1865, he saw a conquered city in ruins. This E. & H. T. Anthony & Company view shows what was left of the Richmond Petersburg Railroad Depot. *(Library of Congress)*

BRASS HOWITZERS (OPPOSITE PAGE)
Two young Union soldiers stand next to two captured Confederate brass mountain howitzers in Richmond in April 1865. *(Library of Congress)*

TOURING THE RUINS (TOP)

This stereo photograph by Alexander Gardner captures two women dressed in black touring Richmond's ruins on April 8, 1865, five days after the Confederate capital was occupied by Union troops, and one day before Gen. Lee's surrender. *(Library of Congress)*

TREDEGAR IRON WORKS (BOTTOM)

The Tredegar Iron Works in Richmond, which produced more than 1,000 artillery pieces for the Confederate army during the war, survived the final fiery end of the Rebel capital because its owner, Joseph Anderson, hired armed guards to protect the complex. *(Library of Congress)*

FORT SUMTER (OPPOSITE PAGE)

Fort Sumter, the Charleston, South Carolina, birthplace of the conflict, was largely reduced to rubble after four years of bombardment. *(Bob Zeller Collection)*

THE

FINAL MONTHS

Chapter 08

RICHMOND PANORAMA (PREVIOUS PAGES)
A photographer for the E. & H. T. Anthony &
Company made this spectacular two-plate
stereoscopic panorama of the city of Richmond
at the end of the Civil War in April 1865. The
state capitol building, used as the Capitol of
the Confederacy, stands out prominently at left,
peering down on the "Burnt District" of destroyed
factories and businesses along the James River.
(Library of Congress)

WHERE LEE SURRENDERED (OPPOSITE PAGE)
The war effectively ended on April 9, 1865, when
Confederate Gen. Robert E. Lee surrendered to
Union Gen. Ulysses S. Grant in the parlor of this
home, owned by Wilmer McLean, at Appomattox
Court House, Virginia. *(Robin Stanford Collection)*

THE
FINAL MONTHS

Chapter 08

A SHORT-HAIRED LINCOLN
The last-known studio portraits of Lincoln were taken before his second inauguration. In early February, 1865, Lincoln was photographed with his hair cut short, apparently to prepare for the plaster life mask of his face made on February 11. *(Library of Congress)*

FORT SUMTER (OPPOSITE PAGE)
Amidst a moonscape of rubble, workers prepared temporary seating for a ceremony inside Fort Sumter to raise the American flag back over the now-destroyed bastion. *(Library of Congress)*

CHARLESTON HARBOR, APRIL 14, 1865 (TOP)

Union Gen. Robert Anderson had been a major when he surrendered Fort Sumter to Confederate forces. On April 14, 1865, he returned to Charleston Harbor to raise the American flag back over Fort Sumter in a ceremony that included many flag-festooned ships, photographed here from what remained of the parapet. *(Library of Congress)*

WATCHING THE SPECTACLE (BOTTOM)

From the parapet of Fort Sumter, a group of Union officers watches the parade of ships and boats in the harbor before the April 14 ceremony. The fort had remained in Confederate hands until they abandoned Charleston in February 1865. *(Library of Congress)*

FORT SUMTER CEREMONY (OPPOSITE PAGE)

Photographer Jacob Coonley took a series of instantaneous stereo views of the flag-raising ceremony in Fort Sumter for E. & H. T. Anthony & Company, including this shot of the gathering crowd. On this same day, in Washington, DC, the actress Laura Keene prepared for the final evening of *Our American Cousin* at Ford's Theatre. *(Library of Congress)*

CRIME
~OF THE~
CENTURY

Chapter **09**

ONLY DAYS into his second term as president, Lincoln had the worn, tired look of a man who had already served the four years. His wife and associates fretted over his haggard appearance and his health. When Gen. Ulysses S. Grant invited the president to visit his headquarters at City Point, Virginia, Lincoln jumped at the opportunity to get away from Washington.

He stayed in City Point for a week, meeting with Grant and his generals; reviewing troops; riding over fresh battlegrounds outside Petersburg, Virginia, where the dead still lay; and, of course, visiting the wounded. Mary and Tad came with him, and they all reunited with Robert, whom Grant had recently appointed to his staff as a

FORD'S THEATRE
The play had already begun as President and Mrs. Lincoln arrived at Ford's Theatre at about 8:30 P.M. on April 14, 1865, but the actors paused, and the band struck up "Hail to the Chief." *(Robin Stanford Collection)*

captain. Despite a nasty, embarrassing outburst from his wife, who went home early, Lincoln thoroughly enjoyed the visit. After a week, when the time came to return to Washington, he lingered, and when Secretary of War Edwin Stanton assured him that all was well in the capital, the president stayed on. The climactic clash of the armies seemed near, and Lincoln wanted to be there for it.

On Sunday, April 2, 1865, with Lincoln watching from a distance, the Union army overwhelmed the Confederate defenders around Petersburg, and Gen. Robert E. Lee began his final westward retreat deeper into Virginia, where the end would come at the tiny village of Appomattox Court House. Confederate President Jefferson Davis was called out of church in Richmond to receive Lee's urgent message to evacuate the now-unprotected capital city. The next day, Union troops marched into a city still ablaze from the fires set by the fleeing Confederates. On April 4, Lincoln decided to take a look himself.

Lincoln and his party came up the James River, switched to
a small boat to navigate the debris-choked river channel, and
entered the city near Libby Prison. Newly freed slaves fell to their
knees before him and began following him, as if he was a Pied
Piper. He sat in the parlor of Davis's presidential mansion and
looked at the disarray inside the Confederate capitol, where desks
were overturned and papers were strewn about. A general asked
Lincoln how the conquered Southerners should be handled.
"If I were in your place, I'd let 'em up easy, let 'em up easy,"
Lincoln said.

On April 9, after more than two weeks in the field, Lincoln
returned to Washington, arriving around sundown to find the
capital's streets filled with celebrating citizens and ablaze with
bonfires. The news of Lee's surrender had just arrived. The war
was all but over. The next morning, a large, jubilant crowd and
two or three bands gathered at the White House and Lincoln
bantered with them from a second-floor window, urging the band
to play "Dixie," which he loved. The South, he said, "attempted
to appropriate it, but I insisted yesterday that we fairly captured
it." They came again that afternoon and returned the next day in
even greater numbers, showering the president with wave upon
wave of cheers.

Lincoln gave a formal policy speech from his White House
window that day, discussing the nature of Reconstruction
and how the Confederate states should be admitted back into
the Union. In the audience was John Wilkes Booth, who had
harbored an obsessive hatred of Lincoln long before the president
saw him perform in 1863. When Lincoln spoke of his desire to
extend the vote to educated blacks and those who served in the
army, Booth seethed. He turned to his associates and vowed,

LAURA KEENE (BELOW & OPPOSITE PAGE)
Lincoln was assassinated while watching the light
comedy *Our American Cousin*, which opened
at Laura Keene's New Theatre in New York on
October 15, 1858. It became one of the most
popular plays of the Civil War era, with upwards
of one thousand performances before the fateful
night of April 14, 1865. This hand-tinted view of
Keene and her co-stars dates to the first week of
December 1858, as documented by the playbill,
shown right side up below. *(Keith Brady Collection)*

AFTER FOUR LONG YEARS
This Gardner studio portrait of the aging
president was long thought to have been one
of the last photos of Lincoln, taken only days
before his assassination. It was actually taken
on February 5, 1865, about a month before the
second inauguration. *(Courtesy of the Center
for Civil War Photography)*

JOHN WILKES BOOTH
The actor John Wilkes Booth, who fired the fatal derringer shot into Lincoln's head, was captured in this portrait taken at the Charles D. Fredericks studio in New York City around 1862. (*John J. Richter Collection*)

Chapter **09**

PRESIDENTIAL BOX (TOP)
& LINCOLN'S CHAIR (BOTTOM)

Lincoln and his party settled into the presidential box, and the president took a seat in his chair. At about 10:15 P.M., John Wilkes Booth put a derringer behind Lincoln's head and fired the fatal shot. Booth jumped from the box to the stage, but his spur caught the decorative flag, and he landed awkwardly, breaking his leg. *(Library of Congress)*

WHERE HE DIED (OPPOSITE PAGE)

Lincoln was carried across the street to the Petersen House, a boarding house, where he died at 7:22 A.M. on April 15, 1865, in a too-short bed that filled much of a tiny back room. This view shows a postwar re-creation of the room. *(John J. Richter Collection)*

"That is the last speech he will ever make." For months, Booth had been plotting to kidnap the president and hold him hostage in exchange for Confederate prisoners and, hopefully, to force the Union to sue for peace. When that plan proved unworkable, Booth decided to shoot him instead.

April 14, 1865—Good Friday—was one of the happiest days of Lincoln's presidency, starting with Robert's return from the front in time for breakfast at the White House. The president was cheerful at his Cabinet meeting, and he talked with fascination about a dream he'd had the night before where he was on a ship "moving with great rapidity towards an indefinite shore." Lincoln said he'd had the same dream preceding the bombardment of Fort Sumter, and the battles of Bull Run, Antietam, Gettysburg, Stones River, Vicksburg, and others, adding that "we shall, judging from the past, have great news very soon." Visitors that day remembered how happy he was, and on an afternoon carriage ride with Mary, he was light-hearted and almost playful, she recalled; she had never seen him so "supremely cheerful."

That evening, as he had at least nine times before, Lincoln went to Ford's Theatre. He was accompanied by his wife, her friend Clara Harris, and Clara's fiancé, Maj. Henry Rathbone, and they settled into the presidential box to see Laura Keene star in *Our American Cousin*, a light comedy that was one of the most popular plays during the Civil War era.

As an actor, Booth was intimately familiar with Ford's Theatre and was easily able to circumvent the president's guards. Meanwhile, Booth's associate, Lewis Powell, a rawboned, blindly loyal Confederate veteran, gained entry to William Seward's residence and savagely stabbed the face and neck of the secretary

of state, who was already badly injured and bedridden from a serious carriage accident. Seward's two sons and two others were injured trying to stop Powell. Back at Ford's Theatre, as the play came to one of its most humorous lines, Booth slipped into the presidential box, leveled his derringer behind Lincoln's right ear and, as the audience roared with laughter, pulled the trigger.

Lincoln's funeral lasted twenty days; the long mournful cortege by train headed back to Springfield, Illinois, pausing in each of the cities where Lincoln had stopped on his way to Washington in 1861. His body first lay in state in the Capitol rotunda, and then the black-draped train pulled out of Washington and headed north to Harrisburg and Philadelphia. Willie's remains were exhumed from a temporary grave in a Georgetown cemetery and put on the train with his father's body. Mary, shattered and grief-stricken yet again, remained bedridden in the White House.

As thousands passed by Lincoln's open coffin in New York City Hall, a desperate Booth, accompanied by co-conspirator David Herold, finally managed to get across the Potomac River into Virginia. Federal cavalrymen were not far behind, carrying card photographs of Booth and Herold to show to the people they encountered. As the funeral train stopped in Buffalo on April 26, Booth was cornered in a tobacco barn on the farm of Richard Garrett and mortally shot in the neck, taking his last breaths on the porch of the Garrett home. On went the funeral train,

WASHINGTON FUNERAL
As Lincoln's funeral procession proceeded down Pennsylvania Avenue on April 19, photographer Alexander Gardner took this rooftop 3-D view.
(Library of Congress)

to Cleveland and Columbus, Indianapolis and Chicago, finally reaching Springfield on May 3. The following day, after thousands had passed by his body in the bunting-draped Illinois statehouse, Lincoln was buried, along with his son, in a vault built into the side of a small hill in Oak Ridge Cemetery.

TREASURY BUILDING (TOP)
Lincoln's assassination was the most shocking, grief-inducing event the young country had ever experienced. Flags flew at half staff, and Washington's official buildings, including the Treasury Building, were decorated with black bunting. *(Robin Stanford Collection)*

IN SAN FRANCISCO (BOTTOM)
In cities coast to coast, mourners honored their "martyred" president with elaborate ceremonies, including this vast parade in San Francisco. *(Robin Stanford Collection)*

PHILADELPHIA FUNERAL (OPPOSITE PAGE)
On April 22, Philadelphia held its own procession on Broad Street. Each city created its own elaborate horse-drawn hearse. *(John J. Richter Collection)*

THE NEW YORK FUNERAL
In this George Stacy stereograph of the New York
funeral procession, the soldiers are holding their
rifles butt-end up. *(Library of Congress)*

LINCOLN IN DEATH

The sole surviving image of Abraham Lincoln in
death is only a half-stereo print. The photo was
undoubtedly originally taken as a stereo view,
since photographer Jeremiah Gurney's two test
shots were in stereo. Here, for the first time, is the
historic last photo of Lincoln presented in 3-D, as
reconstructed from the half-stereo photo by Ron
Labbe of Studio 3D, Maynard, Massachusetts.
*(The Abraham Lincoln Presidential and
Library Museum)*

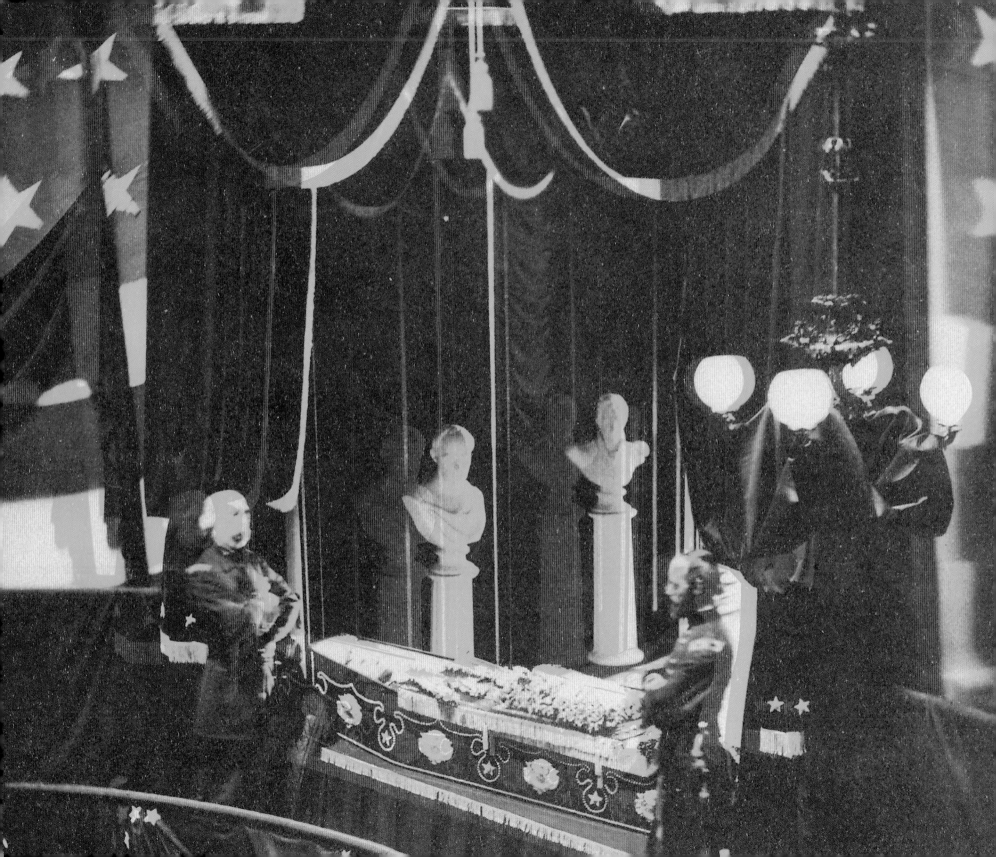

FUNERAL IN COLUMBUS (TOP)

A Columbus, Ohio, photographer took this remarkable stereo view of Lincoln's casket being carried by pallbearers into the Ohio Statehouse on April 29. *(Michael Griffith Collection)*

LINCOLN HOME (BOTTOM)

After a stop in Chicago, the twenty-day funeral procession finally arrived in Springfield, Illinois, where the Lincoln home was draped in black-and-white mourning cloth. *(Robin Stanford Collection)*

TEDDY ROOSEVELT WATCHES (OPPOSITE PAGE)

This hand-colored E. & H. T. Anthony & Company instantaneous view of the New York funeral shows the four-story brownstone owned by the Roosevelt family. One of those watching from the third-floor window is six-year-old Theodore Roosevelt. *(John J. Richter Collection)*

SPRINGFIELD MOURNERS (TOP)

Mourners in Springfield lined up to view Lincoln's
body in the Illinois Statehouse. The African
American man holding the cane is the Rev. Henry
Brown, who had done odd jobs for the Lincolns.
He led the slain president's old horse during
the procession. *(Robin Stanford Collection)*

OAK RIDGE CEMETERY GATE (OPPOSITE PAGE)
LINCOLN'S TEMPORARY TOMB (BOTTOM)

The final procession came through the Oak Ridge
Cemetery gate, before the mourners gathered
on a hot spring day for a graveside service at
Lincoln's temporary receiving tomb.
(John J. Richter Collection)

END OF AN ERA

Chapter 10

THE END OF THE WAR came in stages, first with Lee's surrender on April 9, 1865, and then with the capitulation of Gen. Joseph Johnston and his army on April 26 in North Carolina. As Lincoln was laid to rest in Springfield on May 4, Confederate Gen. Richard Taylor met with Union commanders in Alabama and surrendered his Deep South forces, even as skirmishes and small clashes continued elsewhere. Jefferson Davis was captured in Georgia on May 10, and two days later Yankees fought Confederate forces in the last land engagement, a desultory affair out in Texas that was, ironically, a Southern victory.

Although one more small Confederate army remained in the field (it would surrender on May 26), Union soldiers by the thousands now streamed into Washington for a final victory march down Pennsylvania Avenue. On a bright, sunny May 23, the Army of the Potomac made its way down the broad avenue, with the gleaming bayonets of the tight-packed infantrymen sparkling in the sunlight, interspersed with the prancing horses of the cavalry, the artillery, the engineers, and even the ambulance wagons. The Grand Review continued the following day with the armies of the west until more than 150,000 in all had marched from the Capitol to the White House.

But untold thousands, as Lincoln himself, had not made it to see these two triumphant days. Graveyards north and south swelled with the dead, and countless men among those who survived the horrors of the battlefield would struggle for the rest of their lives without an arm or a leg, or with a minié ball still lodged somewhere in their body.

THE GRAND REVIEW
Infantrymen from the Twentieth Corps of Gen. William T. Sherman's army march down Pennsylvania Avenue on May 24, 1865, the second day of the Grand Review of the Armies. *(Library of Congress)*

END OF AN ERA

Chapter **10**

BOOTH AND HIS ASSOCIATES

A 3-D montage shows facsimile card photographs of John Wilkes Booth and his co-conspirators, all of whom except Booth are shown in photographs taken after their capture. *(Stereo photo illustration by John J. Richter)*

Chapter **10**

BOSTON CORBETT

Religious zealot Boston Corbett, a Union sergeant, claimed to have fired the shot that killed Booth at the Garrett Farm near Port Royal, Virginia, on April 26, 1865. *(Library of Congress)*

ANDREW JOHNSON (THIS PAGE)
A new man, Vice President Andrew Johnson, became the seventeenth president of the United States. *(John J. Richter Collection)*

JOHNSON AND WELLES (OPPOSITE PAGE)
A Tennessee Democrat, Johnson was the only senator from a seceded state to remain in his seat. He was tapped by Lincoln as his running mate to help attract Democratic votes. This candid image shows Johnson with Gideon Welles, Lincoln's secretary of the navy. *(Michael Griffith Collection)*

In the unimaginable shock of the assassination, Lincoln the man instantly became Lincoln the icon. But the man left behind a real family that was now thoroughly devastated by personal tragedy. Mary Lincoln remained at the White House for six weeks after her husband's death, while the new president Andrew Johnson worked out of an office in the Treasury Building. Mary, who had permanent emotional scars from Willie's death, never recovered from her husband's murder either, and dressed only in widow's clothes for the rest of her days. Her youngest son, Tad, became her constant companion, and they moved to Europe in 1868, staying two and a half years. Shortly after their return, though, Tad fell ill, apparently from tuberculosis, and died in 1871. With all of her family dead save Robert, she drifted into insanity, longing for death, which did not come for another eleven years.

In Washington, at the same time that the Grand Review was enthralling the city, a trial was under way of the seven men and one woman who were charged as co-conspirators with Booth in the assassination plot. The proceedings were conducted in a makeshift courtroom at the Old Penitentiary Building on the Arsenal grounds (now Fort McNair) along the Potomac River about twenty blocks south of the Mall. The trial dragged on through the rest of May and nearly all of June, with more than four hundred witnesses, but nary a word allowed from any of the accused. Finally, on July 6, the defendants were told they had been convicted, and four of them—Powell, Herold, George Atzerodt, and Mary Surratt—were told that on the following day they would be taken outside and hanged by the neck until dead.

July 7, 1865, was a hot, sticky day in Washington, and down at the Arsenal a wooden scaffold wide enough for four was nailed together by morning. When the doomed conspirators shuffled

into the sunlight before a crowd of several hundred military men, reporters, and civilians, they could see their own deep, freshly dug graves, and the four simple wooden coffins that awaited their bodies. Alexander Gardner was there, as he had been at so many other historic occasions during the war, and the lenses of his cameras—both stereo and single—were pointed toward the scaffold from the second-floor windows of the penitentiary workshop.

As the death warrants were read, and the nooses were adjusted around the necks of the condemned, Gardner and his associates exposed glass-plate negatives as quickly as possible, capturing at least five 3-D images and six regular photos of the gruesome spectacle. Photography had progressed during the war, along with weaponry, battle tactics, bridge building, and so many other things, and now Gardner was shooting news events as they happened. Today, his photos of the execution, when viewed one after the other, appear like frames of a crude movie, even though the movie camera would not be invented for another thirty years.

The final drama of the Civil War—the condemned on the scaffold, including the first woman ever hanged in the United States—thus came to be etched in the memories of the millions who have seen these images. The end of an era had finally arrived, but its consequences would send aftershocks through the country for more than a century to come. In the wake of

THE PRESIDENTIAL BOX

After the Grand Review, a crowd gathered in front of the presidential viewing stand, where President Andrew Johnson watched from the seat where Lincoln would have sat. *(Library of Congress)*

Lincoln's assassination, the country embarked on a rocky period of Reconstruction under the leadership of President Andrew Johnson. The Northern radicals were even more bent on revenge after Lincoln's murder than they had been when he was still alive. Johnson, a Tennessee native, resisted efforts to grant the full rights of the Constitution to African Americans and vetoed the first Civil Rights bill, which would have extended full citizenship to blacks. He was impeached by Northern Republicans, but managed to keep his job because the 35–19 vote in favor of conviction fell one shy of the required two-thirds majority.

Eventually, though, Southern Democrats would regain enough control in Washington to steer the South back toward a racially divided society that subjugated African Americans and left them without the basic rights guaranteed by the Constitution. Almost a century after the Civil War, the simmering pot of racial inequality would boil over again, this time as the Civil Rights movement. By then, Lincoln would be remembered with his own memorial on the far end of the Mall from the Capitol, and in 1963, the centennial year of the Gettysburg Address, the voice of a black preacher, Martin Luther King Jr., himself destined to be assassinated, would ring forth from the shrine to lead the nation in its struggle to shed the last vestiges of a society in which one human being could own another.

GRAND REVIEW SPECTATORS
You stare into the faces of Civil War Americans in this Alexander Gardner stereo view of spectators in a temporary grandstand erected next to U.S. Capitol for the Grand Review. *(Library of Congress)*

Chapter 10

ARRIVAL ON THE SCAFFOLD (TOP)

After a trial that lasted for almost two months, four conspirators—Mary Surratt, David Herold, Lewis Powell, and George Atzerodt—were sentenced to hang on July 7, 1865. They were told of their fate only the day before. From the second-floor window of an adjacent building, Alexander Gardner took at least five stereo photographs of the hanging, including this view, entitled "The Arrival on the Scaffold." *(Jeffrey Kraus Collection)*

THE DROP (BOTTOM)

The moment of the hanging was caught in this remarkable Alexander Gardner view entitled "The Drop." Surratt, Herold, Powell, and Atzerodt are blurred in the moment of death as they swing in their nooses. *(Library of Congress)*

THE SUSPENSION (OPPOSITE)

In the stifling July heat, Alexander Gardner took this stereo photograph after the bodies had stopped moving. He called it "The Suspension." *(Library of Congress)*

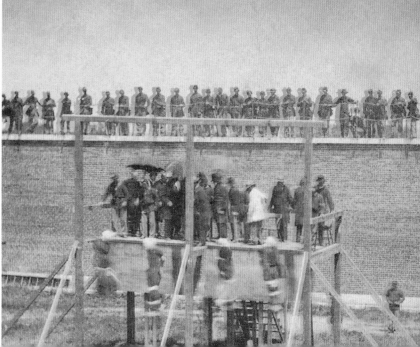

THE LINCOLN TOMB
In 1874, Lincoln was interred in an elaborate new tomb at Oak Ridge Cemetery in Springfield. Today, the cemetery is the second-most visited graveyard in the United States, surpassed only by Arlington National Cemetery. (*John J. Richter Collection*)

Chapter **10**

LINCOLN SARCOPHAGUS (THIS PAGE)

After the new tomb was built, Lincoln's remains were first kept in this marble sarcophagus in the burial room, but after thieves tried to steal the body for ransom in 1876, it was removed and eventually reburied, with Mary Todd Lincoln's remains, under the burial room floor. *(John J. Richter Collection)*

DISABLED SOLDIERS (OPPOSITE PAGE)

The war was over, but tens of thousands of survivors suffered its effects for the rest of their lives. In this tinted view, two Union veterans sell candy and lemonade in Boston Common. The uppermost sign on the tree reads, "Patronize a Disabled Soldier." *(Bob Zeller Collection)*

"A MARVELOUS COLLECTION"

*The following text appears on the reverse of the original stereo view
of the photograph on the opposite page.*

NO. 1. Sofa, an old-fashioned, three-chair-back pattern, mahogony [*sic*],
hair cloth upholstered, and elaborately curved and carved.

NO. 2. Case containing cartoons of the 1860 campaign.

NO. 3. Case containing 91 lives of Lincoln by various authors. 200
autograph manuscripts, reminiscences of Lincoln by noted persons.

NO. 4. Case containing 150 sermons, 35 eulogies, 54 magazines,
76 pamphlets, addresses, etc., on the life of Lincoln.

NO. 5. Mr. Oldroyd made a trip to New Salem, Menard County
(Illinois), found the old home in which Lincoln's earlier manhood
days was spent and purchased it. From a hewed oak log in this
house he had (this) rustic table or stand made, bolted with silver-
plated bolts, and upon this on an elaborate and highly finished
top, is the mourning marble slab. . . .

NO. 6. Statuette of John Rogers of New York, entitled "The
Council of War," presented by him to the collection. It represents
Lincoln seated with a war map . . . Grant is on his right . . .
explaining something to Stanton, who is wiping his glasses with
a handkerchief and looking on the map.

NO. 8. Bust, designed by Jones, at Springfield, Ill., 1861.

NO. 13. The family kitchen stove. "Royal Oak" pattern.

NO. 14. Cradle in which "Robert,'" "Willie" and "Tad" were rocked.

NO. 15. Case containing 240 medals, 171 varieties: copper,
bronze, gilt, brass, pewter, nickel, silver and gold.

NO. 16. Settee made for Mr. Lincoln by a citizen of Springfield, Ill.

NO. 19. Old cane seat chair.

NO. 22. The eagle and wreath which were on the catafalque from
Washington to Springfield.

NO. 33. Bust by Leonard W. Volk, the Chicago sculptor, and
presented by him to this collection. It was cast before the election
in 1860.

Steel-plate engravings of Lincoln are very numerous, and represent
him in all positions and circumstances—surrounded by his family,
by his cabinet, by his generals, by diplomats, in the opera house with
Booth at his back, in the sick room, and the last scene of his life.

There are fifty mourning badges of all kinds. Field surveying notes,
made Nov. 17th, 1836. A piece of blue check, a part of a former
coat worn by Lincoln, given by Mrs. Lincoln to Mrs. Denkle in
1854. Four single pieces of rope, from the ropes that hung Atzerott
[sic], Payne, Harrold [sic], and Mrs. Surratt. A can of tomatoes,
"Lincoln Brand," and several packages of "Uncle Abe" smoking
tobacco. Beer, whiskey and cigar stamps with Lincoln's picture.
The 6, 15 and 90 cent, and a 25-cent newspaper postage stamp.
A shaving from the coffin. Over 100 newspapers with rules turned.

O.H. Oldroyd
State Custodian, Lincoln Homestead, Springfield, Illinois.

LINCOLN HOME MUSEUM (OPPOSITE PAGE)

In 1883, Civil War veteran Osborn Oldroyd rented
Lincoln's Springfield, Illinois, home to display his
massive collection of Lincoln memorabilia. One
reviewer said that it resembled a junk shop. Robert
Lincoln was so appalled that he forced Oldroyd
out in 1893. Oldroyd moved to Washington, DC,
where he rented the Petersen House and set up
his collection there. *(John J. Richter Collection)*

NOTES

PROLOGUE

pg 08 "Discoveries and Inventions.": A new appraisal can be found in Jason Emerson, *Lincoln the Inventor* (Carbondale, IL: Southern Illinois University Press, 2008).

pg 08 "too good a thing": Abraham Lincoln to George D. Ramsay, March 10, 1864, to Edwin M. Stanton and Gideon Welles, February 16, 1863, in Roy P. Basler, ed., *The Collected Works of Abraham Lincoln,* 8 vols. (New Brunswick, NJ: Rutgers University Press, 1953–1955), 7:236; 6:107.

pg 08 "elder-stalk squirts, charged with rose water.": Lincoln to Cuthbert Bullitt, July 28, 1862, *The Collected Works of Abraham Lincoln,* 5:346.

pg 08 "sun pictures": Thomas Hicks, recalling his visit to paint Lincoln's portrait in Springfield, Illinois, in Allen Thorndike Rice, ed., *Reminiscences of Abraham Lincoln by Distinguished Men of His Times* (New York: North American Publishing Co., 1885), 596–597. Seeing one dark-looking early photograph hanging on Lincoln's wall, Hicks joked, "it does not appear to have any sun in it."

pg 08 "multiply copies indefinitely": Lincoln to Harvey G. Eastman, April 7, 1860, *The Collected Works of Abraham Lincoln,* 4:39.

pg 08 "Brady . . . made me President.": Mathew Brady quoted in George Alfred Townsend, "Still Taking Pictures," *New York World*, April 12, 1891, in Mary Panzer, *Mathew Brady and the Image of History* (Washington, DC: Smithsonian Institution Press, 1997), 224.

pg 11 "the best that I have yet seen.": Lincoln to Alexander Gardner, August 18, 1863, in Roy P. Basler, ed., *The Collected Works of Abraham Lincoln: Supplement, 1832–1865* (Westport, CT: Greenwood Press, 1974), 199.

pg 11 . . . *that he had ever seen*.: Michael Burlingame and John R. Turner Ettlinger, eds., *Inside Lincoln's White House: The Complete Civil War Diary of John Hay* (Carbondale, IL: Southern Illinois University Press, 1997), 109.

pg 12 . . . *because the war had ended at last*.: See, for example, the date ascribed to the picture in Stefan Lorant, *Lincoln: A Picture Story of His Life*, rev. ed. (New York: W. W. Norton, 1969), 326.

pg 12 . . . *not on April 10 but on February 5*: William J. Sims, "Matthew Henry Wilson, 1814–1892," *Connecticut Historical Society Bulletin* 37 (October 1972): 109–111.

pg 12 . . . *the portico of the White House on March 6, 1865*: Lloyd Ostendorf, *Lincoln's Photographs: A Complete Album* (Dayton, OH: Rockywood Press, 1998), 412.

pg 13 "the fuel of interest to the fire of genius.": Reprinted in Emerson, *Lincoln the Inventor*, 78.

INTRODUCTION

pg 16 "No painting or engraving ever approached it.": Samuel F. B. Morse to *New-York Observer,* April 20, 1839; *New-York Observer* 17, no. 16 (April, 20 1839): 62.

pg 16 . . . *with the same resolute countenance.*: The date of the first sitting is established in Charles Hamilton and Lloyd Ostendorf, *Lincoln in Photographs: An Album of Every Known Pose* (Dayton, OH: Morningside, 1985), 4–5.

pg 20 . . . *at least 150 different photographs* . . . : this tally includes 132 extant images and 18 documented images that are missing or destroyed. Of the extant images, 126 are documented by Hamilton and Ostendorf in *Lincoln in Photographs*. The other six consist of the two images of Lincoln at Gettysburg featured in this book, an image of Lincoln at Gettysburg owned by William A. Frassanito and published in his *Early Photography at Gettysburg* (Gettysburg, PA: Thomas, 1995), two stereo photographs of the second inauguration, both featured in this volume, and one additional stereograph of the first inauguration.

pg 23 "as if they would scratch our eyes out.": Oliver Wendell Holmes, "The Stereoscope and the Stereograph," *Atlantic Monthly*, no. 3 (June 1859); as reprinted in *Soundings from the Atlantic* (Boston, MA: Ticknor and Fields, 1864), 148.

CHAPTER 1: AN UPSET VICTORY

pg 27 "altogether uncomely face.": Henry Villard, "Recollections of Lincoln," *Atlantic Monthly* 93, no. 556 (February 1904): 165–174.

pg 28 . . . *anathema to the South.*: See appraisal of Cooper Union photograph in Harold Holzer, *Lincoln at Cooper Union* (New York: Simon & Schuster, 2004), 88–96.

pg 28 . . . *listened to a drunk sing "Dixie"* . . . : Stephen B. Oates, *With Malice Toward None: A Life of Abraham Lincoln* (New York: Harper Perennial, 1994), 212.

pg 32 . . . *on a 1,904-mile train trip,* . . . : David Herbert Donald, *Lincoln* (New York: Simon & Schuster, 1995), 272.

pg 32 "When I entered the room . . ." Hamilton and Ostendorf, *Lincoln in Photographs*, 1977.

pg 32 ". . . by the better angels of our nature.": First Inaugural Address—Final Text, *The Collected Works of Abraham Lincoln,* 4:262–271.

pg 37 "The wretched hovels": Laura M. Towne diary entry for May 23, 1862, "Diary of Laura M. Towne," Penn School Papers, The Southern Historical Collection, Wilson Library, University of North Carolina at Chapel Hill, transcript pages 33–62.

CHAPTER 2: LINCOLN BECOMES PRESIDENT

pg 45 "before an expedition could be sent to their relief.": Michael Burlingame, ed., *With Lincoln in the White House: Letters, Memoranda, and Other Writings of John G. Nicolay,* 1860–1865 (Carbondale, IL: Southern Illinois University Press, 2006), 46–47 (Memorandum, July 3, 1861).

pg 46 "all the troubles and anxieties of his life": Theodore Calvin Pease and James G. Randall, eds., *The Diary of Orville Hickman Browning, Volume I, 1850–1864* (Springfield, IL: Illinois State Historical Library, 1925), 476.

pg 48 (caption) "The people of this great town:" *The Illustrated London News*, Volume 38, Number 1089, May 18, 1861, 467.

pg 50 . . . *the "Stars and Bars" would fly* . . . : James Ford Rhodes, *History of the United States from the Compromise of 1850, Vol. 3, 1860–1862* (New York: Harper & Brothers, 1900), 361.

pg 50 "in picturesque bivouac": John G. Nicolay and John Hay, *Abraham Lincoln, a History* (New York: The Century Co., 1890), 4:107.

pg 50 "You are the only real thing.": Ibid., 152–153.

CHAPTER 3: 1862 AND THE BATTLE OF ANTIETAM

pg 62 "the bottom is out of the tub!": Carl Sandburg, *Abraham Lincoln: The War Years 1861–1865* (New York: Dell Publishing Co., 1924), 533.

pg 62 "almost ready to hang himself.": Doris Kearns Goodwin, *Team of Rivals: The Political Genius of Abraham Lincoln* (New York: Simon & Schuster, 2005), 479.

pg 62 "Please do not let him get off. . . .": Telegram, Lincoln to George B. McClellan, September 12, 1862, *The Collected Works of Abraham Lincoln*, 5:418.

pg 72 "every word is so closely noted . . .": Speech at Frederick, Maryland, October 4, 1862, *The Collected Works of Abraham Lincoln*, 5:450.

pg 72 "little sad song": Ward Hill Lamon, Memorandum Concerning Ward H. Lamon and the Antietam Episode, ca. September 12, 1864, *The Collected Works of Abraham Lincoln*, 7:550.

pg 72 "my own estimate of myself": Ward Hill Lamon, Dorothy Lamon Teillard, *Recollections of Abraham Lincoln 1847–1865* (Chicago: A. C. McClurg and Company, 1895), 142.

CHAPTER 4: WASHINGTON AT WAR

pg 76 "I have made no mistake.": reply to Serenade in Honor of Emancipation Proclamation, Sept. 24, 1862, *The Collected Works of Abraham Lincoln*, 5:438.

pg 76 "and sloughs for roads.": Henry Adams, *The Education of Henry Adams* (Sioux Falls, SD: NuVision Publications, 2007 reprint), 82.

pg 76 "even with the admixture of alcohol.": G. W. Bagby, "Washington City," *Atlantic Monthly*, January 1861, as reprinted in Marcus Benjamin, ed. *Washington During War Time* (Washington, DC: The National Tribune Co., 1902), 8.

pg 78 "an old and unsuccessful hotel.": Goodwin, *Team of Rivals*, 359.

pg 78 (caption) "Can it be taken with a single negative?": Hamilton and Ostendorf, *Lincoln in Photographs*, 129.

pg 81 "twenty thousand drowned cats": William Roscoe Thayer, *John Hay* (Boston and New York: Houghton Mifflin Co., 1915), 147.

CHAPTER 5: GETTYSBURG

pg 97 "They wish to get rid of me": Pease, ed., *The Diary of Orville Hickman Browning,* I:600.

pg 98 "What will the country say!": Noah Brooks, *Washington in Lincoln's Time* (New York: The Century Co., 1895), 58.

pg 98 "the rebellion will be over.": Telegram, Abraham Lincoln to Henry W. Halleck, July 7, 1863, *The Collected Works of Abraham Lincoln*, 6:319.

pg 98 "and they would not close it.": Donald, *Lincoln,* 446.

pg 98 "I am distressed immeasurably because of it.": Unsent letter, Abraham Lincoln to George W. Meade, July 14, 1863, *The Collected Works of Abraham Lincoln*, 6:327–329.

pg 98 "every general in the field a barrel of it.": Francis Bicknell Carpenter, *The Inner Life of Abraham Lincoln: Six Months at the White House* (New York: Hurd and Houghton, 1872), 247.

pg 98 "if I *had* said it.": Oates, *With Malice Toward None*, 354.

pg 108 "he was in very good spirits.": Ibid., 134.

pg 114 "short, short, short": Brooks, *Washington in Lincoln's Time*, 286.

pg 114 "Four score and seven years ago": Address Delivered at the Dedication of the Cemetery at Gettysburg, November 19, 1863, *The Collected Works of Abraham Lincoln*, 7:22–23.

pg 114 "as you did in two minutes.": Goodwin, *Team of Rivals*, 586.

CHAPTER 6: LINCOLN AND HIS FAMILY

pg 117 "generous beyond anything I have ever known": Ibid., 351.

pg 118 "working on a flat boat": Donald, *Lincoln*, 42.

pg 120 "from this hideous nightmare?": Goodwin, *Team of Rivals*, 593.

pg 125 (caption) "perfectly lawless": Charles W. Moores, *The Life of Abraham Lincoln for Boys and Girls* (Boston and New York: Houghton Mifflin Co., 1909), 109.

CHAPTER 7: 1864—A YEAR OF ALL-OUT WAR

pg 137 "as gloom was last winter.": Goodwin, *Team of Rivals,* 598.

pg 137 "there will be no turning back.": Jean Edward Smith, *Grant* (New York: Simon & Schuster, 2001), 334.

pg 138 "poured out their blood for the Union cause.": Gideon Welles, *The Diary of Gideon Welles (In Three Volumes)* (Boston and New York: Houghton Mifflin Co., 1911), II:44.

pg 138 "one of the most terrible": Speech at Great Central Sanitary Fair, Philadelphia, June 16, 1864, *The Collected Works of Abraham Lincoln*, 7:394–396.

pg 144 "this Administration will not be re-elected.": Memorandum Concerning His Probable Failure of Re-election, August 23, 1864, *The Collected Works of Abraham Lincoln*, 7:514–515.

pg 144 "how *strong* we still are.": Response to a Serenade, November 10, 1864, *The Collected Works of Abraham Lincoln*, 8:101.

pg 146 (caption) "accumulating overwhelming numbers.": Douglas Southall Freeman, *R. E. Lee: A Biography* (New York and London: Charles Scribner's Sons, 1934), 459.

pg 146 (caption) "without parallel in the civilized world.": "A Talk with Gen. R. E. Lee," *New York Times*, August 12, 1879, page 3.

pg 147 (caption) "man of much dignity": Ulysses S. Grant, *Personal Memoirs of U. S. Grant: In Two Volumes* (New York: Charles L. Webster & Co., 1885), 489.

pg 149 (caption) "When I get all the kinks out": Hamilton and Ostendorf, *Lincoln in Photographs*, 118.

CHAPTER 8: THE FINAL MONTHS

pg 153 "about 25,000 bales of cotton.": Telegram, William T. Sherman to Abraham Lincoln, December 22, 1864, Robert Todd Lincoln Collection of the Papers of Abraham Lincoln, Washington, DC: Library of Congress.

pg 153 "Many, many thanks for your Christmas gift.": Telegram, Abraham Lincoln to William T. Sherman, December 26, 1864, *The Collected Works of Abraham Lincoln*, 8:181–182.

pg 154 "I could not have done what I have.": Margaret Washington, *Sojourner Truth's America* (Urbana and Chicago, IL; University of Illinois Press, 2009), 315.

pg 154 "in mind, body and nerves a very different man.": Goodwin, *Team of Rivals*, 702.

pg 154 "Speed, I am a little alarmed": Donald, *Lincoln*, 568.

pg 158 "made my heart jump": Noah Brooks, *Abraham Lincoln* (New York: Fred DeFau & Co., 1888), 412–413.

pg 158 "With malice toward none": Second Inaugural Address, March 4, 1865, *The Collected Works of Abraham Lincoln*, 8:332–333.

pg 158 "white men is in class number one": Donald, *Lincoln*, 520–21.

pg 158 "I have not come for the play": Rufus Rockwell Wilson, *Intimate Memories of Lincoln* (Elmira, NY: Primavera Press, 1945), 424–425.

CHAPTER 9: CRIME OF THE CENTURY

pg 174 "I'd let 'em up easy.": Helen Nicolay, *Personal Traits of Abraham Lincoln* (New York: The Century Co., 1912), 224.

pg 174 "we fairly captured it.": Response to Serenade, April 10, 1865, *The Collected Works of Abraham Lincoln*, 8:393–394.

pg 180 "the last speech he will ever make.": Donald, *Lincoln,* 588.

pg 180 "towards an indefinite shore.": Welles, *The Diary of Gideon Welles*, II:282–283.

pg 180 "supremely cheerful.": Waldo Emerson Reck, *A. Lincoln, His Last 24 Hours* (Jefferson, NC: McFarland & Co., 1987), 47.

CHAPTER 10: END OF AN ERA

pg 198 ". . . dressed only in widow's clothes.": Philip B. Kunhardt, Jr., Philip B. Kunhardt III, and Peter W. Kunhardt, *Lincoln: An Illustrated Biography* (New York: Knopf, 1992), 394.

~ BIBLIOGRAPHY ~

ADAMS, HENRY. *The Education of Henry Adams*, reprint. Sioux Falls, SD: NuVision Publications, 2007.

BAGBY, G. W. "Washington City," *Atlantic Monthly*, January 1861.

BASLER, ROY P., ED. *The Collected Works of Abraham Lincoln*, 8 vols. New Brunswick, NJ: Rutgers University Press, 1953–1955.

BASLER, ROY P., ED. *The Collected Works of Abraham Lincoln: Supplement, 1832–1865.* Westport, CT: Greenwood Press, 1974.

BENJAMIN, MARCUS, ED. *Washington During War Time.* Washington, DC: The National Tribune Company, 1902.

BROOKS, NOAH. *Abraham Lincoln.* New York: Fred DeFau & Company, 1888.

BROOKS, NOAH. *Washington in Lincoln's Time.* New York: The Century Company, 1895.

BURLINGAME, MICHAEL, ED. *With Lincoln in the White House: Letters, Memoranda, and Other Writings of John G. Nicolay, 1860–1865.* Carbondale, IL: Southern Illinois University Press, 2006.

BURLINGAME, MICHAEL, AND JOHN R. TURNER ETTLINGER, EDS. *Inside Lincoln's White House: The Complete Civil War Diary of John Hay.* Carbondale, IL: Southern Illinois University Press, 1997.

CARPENTER, FRANCIS BICKNELL. *The Inner Life of Abraham Lincoln: Six Months at the White House.* New York: Hurd and Houghton, 1872.

DONALD, DAVID HERBERT. *Lincoln.* New York: Simon & Schuster, 1995.

EMERSON, JASON. *Lincoln the Inventor.* Carbondale, IL: Southern Illinois University Press, 2008.

FRASSANITO, WILLIAM A. *Early Photography at Gettysburg.* Gettysburg, PA: Thomas, 1995.

FREEMAN, DOUGLAS SOUTHALL. *R. E. Lee: A Biography.* New York and London: Charles Scribner's Sons, 1934.

GOODWIN, DORIS KEARNS. *Team of Rivals: The Political Genius of Abraham Lincoln.* New York: Simon and Schuster, 2005.

GRANT, ULYSSES S. *Personal Memoirs of U. S. Grant: In Two Volumes.* New York: Charles L. Webster & Company, 1885.

HAMILTON, CHARLES, AND LLOYD OSTENDORF. *Lincoln in Photographs: An Album of Every Known Pose.* Dayton, OH: Morningside, 1985.

HOLMES, OLIVER WENDELL. "The Stereoscope and the Stereograph." Originally published in the *Atlantic Monthly* 3 (1859). In *Soundings from the Atlantic.* Boston, MA: Ticknor and Fields, 1864.

HOLZER, HAROLD. *Lincoln at Cooper Union.* New York: Simon & Schuster, 2004.

KUNHARDT JR., PHILIP B., PHILIP B. KUNHARDT III, AND PETER W. KUNHARDT, *Lincoln: An Illustrated Biography.* New York: Knopf 1992.

LAMON, WARD HILL, AND DOROTHY LAMON TEILLARD. *Recollections of Abraham Lincoln 1847–1865.* Chicago: A. C. McClurg and Company, 1895.

LORANT, STEFAN. *Lincoln: A Picture Story of His Life,* rev. ed. New York: W. W. Norton, 1969.

MOORES, CHARLES. W. *The Life of Abraham Lincoln for Boys and Girls.* Boston and New York: Houghton Mifflin Company, 1909.

NEW YORK TIMES, "A Talk with Gen. R. E. Lee," August 12, 1879.

NICOLAY, HELEN. *Personal Traits of Abraham Lincoln.* New York: The Century Company, 1912.

NICOLAY, JOHN G., AND JOHN HAY. *Abraham Lincoln, a History.* New York: The Century Company, 1890.

OATES, STEPHEN B. *With Malice Toward None: A Life of Abraham Lincoln.* New York: Harper Perennial, 1994.

OSTENDORF, LLOYD. *Lincoln's Photographs: A Complete Album.* Dayton, OH: Rockywood Press, 1998.

PANZER, MARY. *Mathew Brady and the Image of History.* Washington, DC: Smithsonian Institution Press, 1997.

PEASE, THEODORE CALVIN, AND JAMES G. RANDALL, EDS. *The Diary of Orville Hickman Browning, Volume I, 1850–1864.* Springfield, IL: Illinois State Historical Library, 1925.

RECK, WALDO EMERSON. *Abraham Lincoln, His Last 24 Hours.* Jefferson, NC: McFarland & Company, 1987.

RHODES, JAMES FORD. *History of the United States from the Compromise of 1850, Vol. 3, 1860–1862.* New York: Harper & Brothers, 1900.

RICE, ALLEN THORNDIKE, ED. *Reminiscences of Abraham Lincoln by Distinguished Men of His Times.* New York: North American Publishing Company, 1885.

SANDBURG, CARL. *Abraham Lincoln: The War Years 1861–1865.* New York: Dell Publishing Company, 1924.

SCHAFF, MORRIS. *Jefferson Davis: His Life and Personality.* Boston: John W. Luce and Company, 1922.

SHERMAN, WILLIAM T. Telegram to Abraham Lincoln in "Robert Todd Lincoln Collection of the Papers of Abraham Lincoln." Washington, DC: Library of Congress, December 1864.

SIMS, WILLIAM J. "Matthew Henry Wilson, 1814–1892," *Connecticut Historical Society Bulletin* 37 (October 1972).

SMITH, JEAN EDWARD. *Grant.* New York: Simon and
Schuster, 2001.

THAYER, WILLIAM ROSCOE. *John Hay.* Boston and
New York: Houghton Mifflin Company, 1915.

TOWNE, LAURA M. "Diary of Laura M. Towne." Penn
School Papers, The Southern Historical Collection, Wilson
Library, University of North Carolina at Chapel Hill.

TOWNSEND, GEORGE ALFRED. "Still Taking
Pictures," *New York World,* April 12, 1891.

VILLARD, HENRY, "Recollections of Lincoln," *Atlantic
Monthly* 93 (556) February 1904.

WASHINGTON, MARGARET. *Sojourner Truth's America.*
Urbana and Chicago, IL: University of Illinois Press, 2009.

WELLES, GIDEON. *The Diary of Gideon Welles (In
Three Volumes).* Boston and New York: Houghton Mifflin
Company, 1911.

WILSON, RUFUS ROCKWELL. *Intimate Memoirs of
Lincoln.* Elmira, NY: Primavera Press, 1945.

CIVIL WAR PHOTOGRAPHY

A NOTE ABOUT THE PHOTOGRAPHS

All of the photographs in this volume were originally created in a stereoscopic format and most were seen in 3-D by Civil War Americans. The image of Lincoln in his casket exists today only as a single 2-D photograph, but apparently was originally created in 3-D. We have restored its original depth. The portraits herein were taken with a four-lens camera, which produced two side-by-side stereoscopic pairs. In many cases, actual stereo views were never issued of the portraits, and they are presented here for the first time ever as 3-D images. We owe a debt of gratitude to the late Lloyd Ostendorf for pioneering this technique of reassembling stereoscopic images, which he usually did by acquiring different vintage card photographs of the same pose that emanated from the different lenses of the four-lens camera.

Nearly all of the images from the Library of Congress—both portraits and documentary photographs—come from the original glass-plate negatives, most of which are still in remarkably good condition and contain tremendous detail. Beginning in 2001 and continuing through 2003, the Library conducted a comprehensive digitizing project, scanning all of its more than 7,000 negatives, no matter the condition, and making them available as free online downloads at low, high and, ultra-high resolution at www.loc.gov/pictures/collection/cwp.

THE CENTER FOR CIVIL WAR PHOTOGRAPHY

The Center for Civil War Photography (CCWP), founded in 1999, is a nonprofit 501 (c)(3) corporation dedicated to educating people about this fascinating field of Civil War scholarship; promoting the study of its rich variety of formats; preserving original images, equipment, and methods; and presenting visually spectacular interpretive programs and seminars. The Center maintains an active Web site, conducts an annual three-day seminar at different battlefields, publishes soft-cover books of Civil War photos, and produces 3-D shows and exhibitions for museums.

Visit the Center for Civil War Photography at www.civilwarphotography.org.

THE CENTER FOR CIVIL WAR PHOTOGRAPHY
- HISTORY IN FOCUS -

⌇ ACKNOWLEDGMENTS ⌇

Almost half of the 3-D images in this volume come from the original Civil War glass-plate photographic negatives at the Library of Congress. We would like to thank Curator of Photographs Carol Johnson for her invaluable assistance, as well as the staff of the Prints and Photographs Reading Room.

A special thanks to leading Lincoln scholar and author Harold Holzer, senior vice president of external communications at the Metropolitan Museum of Art, for his masterly prologue, his review of the narrative, and his wise counsel on all matters related to Lincoln.

We owe a great debt of gratitude to the private collectors of stereo views who have done so much in our time to reassemble the stereo photographic history of nineteenth-century America. In particular, we want to thank Robin Stanford of Houston, Texas, who has assembled an unparalleled collection of Civil War stereo views, including the many views presented in this volume. Dealer and collector Jeffrey Kraus at Antiquephographics.com, a longtime friend, has contributed five superb views. We also thank collectors Keith Brady, Michael Griffith, and John Weiler for their generous contributions. Special thanks to Ron Labbe at Studio3D.com for restoring 3-D to the sole surviving half-stereo print of Lincoln in his casket at New York City Hall. We also thank Jennifer Ericson at the Abraham Lincoln Library and Museum in Springfield, Illinois, for permission to use the image.

Thanks to Keith Davis, senior curator of photography at the Nelson-Atkins Museum of Art, Kansas City, Missouri, as well as assistant curator of photography Jane L. Aspinwall and department assistants Chelsea Schlievert and Stacey Sherman in Imaging Services for their generosity in letting us publish the stereographs of Lincoln delivering the second inaugural address and Alexander Gardner's Gallery.

In the magical process of turning an idea into a book, we owe special thanks to our literary agent, John Silbersack, executive vice president of Trident Media Group, New York, New York; as well as assistants Emma Beavers and Elizabeth Kellogg. At Chronicle Books, we'd like to thank our editor, Emily Haynes, as well as senior editor Bill LeBlond, Emilie Sandoz, Becca Cohen, and designer Trina Hancock. Thanks also to Garry E. Adelman, vice president of the Center for Civil War Photography, for his thorough review of the manuscript.

We would also like to thank Wm. B. Becker; John Beshears; Susan Boardman; Ron Coddington; Richard Loren Copley; Jeff Fisher of Mercury Press, Inc, Hanover, PA.; William A. Frassanito; Michelle Ganz, archivist at the Abraham Lincoln Library and Museum, Harrogate, TN; Rob Gibson; John Kelley; Jennifer Kon, executive director of the Center for Civil War Photography; Cliff Krainik; Jonathan Mann, publisher of *The Railsplitter*; Erin Carlson Mast, curator and site administrator at President Lincoln's Cottage, Washington, DC; the National Stereoscopic Association; Chet Peters; Ann Shumard, curator of photographs at the Smithsonian Institution's National Portrait Gallery Washington, DC; John Saddy; Tim Smith, Harvey S. Teal; John Waldsmith; Jill Voges; Daniel R. Weinberg and the Abraham Lincoln Book Shop, Chicago, IL; and George S. Whiteley IV.

Finally, and most importantly, Bob Zeller would like to thank his wife, Ann Bailie, and children, Sara and Jesse; and John J. Richter would like to thank his wife, Jody, and children, Edward and Julia. This book is dedicated to them.

INDEX

Italics indicate pages with photographs.